BEFORE FARMING

By the same author:

Life in Copper Age Britain

Warfare in Prehistoric Britain

Sacred Circles: Prehistoric Stone Circles of Wales

Ancient Echoes: The Early History of a Welsh Peninsula

Before Farming
Life in Prehistoric Wales
225000–4000BC

Julian Heath

First published in 2013

© Julian Heath

© Gwasg Carreg Gwalch 2013

Published with the financial support
of the Welsh Books Council

ISBN: 978-1-84527-456-6

Cover design: Eleri Owen, Pwllheli
Cover photo: Cathole Cave (Chris Elphick)

Published by Gwasg Carreg Gwalch,
12 Iard yr Orsaf, Llanrwst, Wales LL26 0EH
tel: 01492 642031
fax: 01492 641502
email: books@carreg-gwalch.com
website: www.carreg-gwalch.com

They are almost too much, the human footprints: looking at them, touching them, felt like eavesdropping, or secretly watching someone in an unguarded moment. I had to stare at them but part of me wanted to look away, out of respect for privacy . . . Our ancient past is powerful magic, strong drink – even a little shot of it can snatch your breath away and make you wonder if you can, any more, believe what you are seeing.

Neil Oliver, *A History of Ancient Britain*

Contents

Introduction

I have to admit that when I first began to think about writing this book, I was a little wary, as I would be entering prehistoric territory that was rather unfamiliar to me. My feet are planted firmly in the later prehistoric landscapes of Wales, rather than those of the earlier Palaeolithic and Mesolithic hunter-gatherers with which this book is concerned. Thus it is the impressive megalithic tombs built by the first farmers in the Neolithic ('New Stone Age'), the mysterious stone circles built by Late Neolithic and Early Bronze Age communities, and the magnificent hillforts of the Iron Age that have continued to cast their spell on me ever since I took my first faltering steps on a now well-trodden path into Welsh prehistory, whilst I was an undergraduate at Liverpool University (several years ago now!).

Nonetheless, realising that I had been rather neglectful of the prehistoric hunter-gatherer communities who roamed the Welsh countryside all those thousands of years ago, living off the bounty that nature provided, I cast aside my wariness and pressed ahead. I was glad that I did so, as writing this book has made me realise that although these people may not have built mighty stone monuments or made beautiful objects of bronze, iron, or gold, this does not lessen their relevance. They, too, have left fascinating traces of their ancient lives which are also worthy of inclusion in the long story of Wales. Of course, it would be hard to deny that the arrival of farming and metalworking ultimately had a profound impact on shaping the modern nation of Wales, but it would also be fair to say that without the hunter-gatherers of the Palaeolithic and Mesolithic, the Welsh nation would never have come into being.

As is the case in many other parts of Europe, the arrival of farming in the Neolithic literally sowed the seeds for the eventual extinction of the hunter-gatherer way of life, which could be said to have first emerged some two and a half million years ago when the earliest humans or 'hominids' learnt to walk upright and make simple stone tools. In Wales, farming arrived around 4000 BC, but farming seems to have emerged first in the Near East about 9000 BC, and from here, it gradually spread west into the rest of Europe.

I should point out, however, that, as in the rest of Europe, the arrival of farming in Wales would not have been a uniform process. In some parts of the country, farming was probably introduced by small groups of immigrants from other parts of Europe, but in others, hunter-gatherers may have adopted farming from these groups or with other early farmers on the continent (and Ireland) with whom they were in contact. Also, it is worth bearing in mind that some hunter-gatherer communities would have made a stand against farming and continued to practice their ancient and traditional way of life alongside the first farmers, perhaps, in some cases, for many hundreds of years. It is also quite probable that relations between the two would not always have been peaceful, with armed conflicts sometimes breaking out for various reasons (e.g. theft of livestock or simply because of an insult). In this respect, it may be worth mentioning that in north-east Belgium, archaeologists have found evidence that immigrant Neolithic farmers built fortified border villages, which lay on the edge of a 'no-man's land' that separated the immigrants from the native hunter-gatherers.

It is sobering to realise that today, the hunter-gatherer way of life, which existed for hundreds of thousands of years around the globe, is now practiced by less than 0.001 per cent of humans, who live in marginal areas such as the

Kalahari Desert of South Africa or the Amazon rain forest. Anthropological studies of these surviving, and less recent, hunter-gatherer societies may provide us with some insights into prehistoric hunter-gatherer communities in Europe. For example, we know that in hunter-gatherer societies which have been studied by anthropologists, there are bands and tribes. The band is the smaller of the two and is formed by single families 'banding' together into one single group, whilst tribes come into being through the union of several bands. Some bands contain less than fifty people, although they have often been found to contain a few hundred people. Unsurprisingly, the number of persons in a tribe is much larger than in a band, and often there can be as many as 1,000 people in a tribe, if not more, as seen with the Native Indians of North America. For example, there were thousands of Navajo Indians, many of whom died when they were forced by the US Army to march to the new reservations in the nineteenth century. Unfortunately, unless a time-machine is invented, we will never be able to know whether both hunter-gatherer bands and tribes existed in Palaeolithic and Mesolithic Wales, or the exact size of them.

If the archaeologist Christopher Smith hits near the mark with his suggestion that in Britain as a whole during the Upper Palaeolithic and Mesolithic there was a population of only some 3,000 to 6,000 people, then it could be the case that there were no prehistoric hunter-gatherer tribes at all, anywhere in Britain; just small bands in various parts of the country. Personally, I feel that there would have been somewhat more people than this in Britain in the Upper Palaeolithic and Mesolithic – although there would certainly have been plenty of room for everyone amongst its landscapes. Interestingly, Smith's population estimates for the Upper Palaeolithic and Mesolithic stand in marked contrast to those made by the noted palaeoanthropologist Clive Gamble, for the Middle Palaeolithic (*c*.300,000–40,000 years ago – the time of the famous Neanderthals). He has suggested that in Britain and Ireland during this period, there could have been as many as 27,000 people living on the two islands.

Before readers are introduced in Chapter One to the important evidence which has been discovered in Wales for perhaps the most enigmatic members of the human species ever to have walked the Earth, I should perhaps say a little more about the Palaeolithic and Mesolithic in Britain, and continental Europe.

The Palaeolithic (or 'Old Stone Age') represents an extremely long-lived chapter in the human story and began in Africa some two and a half million years ago, with the emergence of the earliest humans or 'hominids' of the genus *Homo*. They used simple chopping tools that were fashioned by removing flakes from cobbles and pebbles with hammerstones. It is widely believed that a species of hominid known as *Homo erectus* was the first to spread out of the African homeland to Asia and Europe, although exactly when this happened is a matter of debate. However, it is possible that *Homo erectus* was present in parts of Europe over 1.5 million years ago – if not earlier.

As yet, though, the earliest hominid remains in Britain have come from the famous Lower Palaeolithic site of Boxgrove in Sussex. These date to around half a million years ago and consist of a gnawed tibia bone and two teeth from two individuals who are thought to have belonged to a powerfully-built hominid species known as *Homo heidelbergensis* (after a hominid jawbone that was found near Heidelberg in 1907), which was descended directly from *Homo erectus*. It is widely believed that the famous but much maligned Neanderthals gradually evolved from *Homo heidelbergensis*, and a famous discovery made at Swanscombe in Kent suggests that early Neanderthals may have been present in Britain as early as 400,000 years ago. Here, in the Barnfield Pit disused gravel quarry, three parts of the back of a probable female skull were found in levels dating to this time (it is also worth mentioning that some 100,000 handaxes have been recovered from this area!). One of these skull fragments displays a shallow depression (the *suprainiac fossa*) fragment, which would have formed an anchor point for the neck muscles. This is a characteristic feature of Neanderthal skulls and is not seen on modern human ones, which instead, have a distinctive bump where the neck muscles were attached. Although the front of the Swanscombe skull was missing, judging from other more complete and contemporary examples from elsewhere (e.g. the one found at Steinheim in Germany), it seems probable that it would also have displayed the angled cheekbones and very prominent brow ridges that are such a distinctive feature of Neanderthal skulls. Some palaeoanthropologists feel that the Swanscombe and Steinheim skulls (and other human fossils of the same age) should be classified as 'pre-Neanderthal' rather than 'early Neanderthal' because it is generally felt that 'classic' or fully developed Neanderthal features were only present in human populations living in Europe and western Asia from c.130,000-30,000 years ago.

At this point, I should say something about the different dating conventions used in this book, because as readers will see, dates of archaeological sites and artefacts are expressed as both 'BP' and 'BC'. The term 'BP' stands for 'Before Present' and archaeologists Stephen Aldhouse-Green and Elizabeth Walker have explained why archaeologists use it, better than I ever could:

The term 'BP' is used in a technical sense by archaeologists in the quoting of radiocarbon dates to 'years before AD 1950'. Thus 2000 BC would be expressed as 3950 BP. The year AD 1950 was chosen as it was only shortly before then that the radiocarbon technique was developed. Radiocarbon dates are named after the radioactive isotope of carbon (Carbon-14) whose decay is measured to date the age of the [archaeological] sample in question.

The term 'BC', of course, stands for 'Before Christ'. I should point out that some archaeologists now prefer to avoid using BC because of its religious connotations and instead use 'BCE' ('Before Common Era') or even CE ('Common Era'). However, whether they are religious or not, many archaeologists still use the traditional BC, as I also have done in this book. The reason why archaeologists switch between the two terms in the archaeological literature is basically because 'BP' dates are those that have been determined in the laboratory, but have not yet been 'calibrated' to actual calendar years, as 'BC' dates have. Anybody wishing to look at archaeological dating methods in more detail can easily find information on this subject on the internet.

Although no hominid remains predating the above have so far been found in Britain, there have been some hugely important discoveries that have pushed back the date of the first colonisation of Britain by early humans by many thousands of years. At Happisburgh on the Norfolk coast, butchered animal bones were found with flint 'Acheulian' handaxes and flake tools, in gravel deposits dating to around 800,000 BP, whilst at Pakefield on the Suffolk coast, thirty-two worked flints were discovered in association with the remains of animals that lived around 700,000 years ago. More recently, it is the famous Palaeolithic cave site of Kent's Cavern, near Torquay, that has provided us with skeletal evidence for Britain's oldest modern humans. This consists of a maxilla (upper jaw) fragment with three teeth that has recently been redated from around 31,000 BP, to a more probable 44,000–41,000 BP.

Though Acheulian handaxes are rare in Wales, I'll say more. They are a distinct characteristic of the Lower Palaeolithic (which dates from about 2.5 million to 300,000 years ago) and the early members of our own species. These elaborate 'bifacial' (worked on both sides) and often highly symmetrical tools are teardrop or pear-shaped. They have a wide geographical distribution, being found in China, the Far East, southern Africa, parts of India, and western Europe. They were made on large pieces or 'flakes' struck from boulders of flint, chert, obsidian, lava or quartzite, which were then further refined into their finished form by the removal of smaller flakes, with flakes also being removed from the tips and edges to provide sharp cutting edges. The manufacture of a handaxe was not a straightforward task and would have required a fair amount of skill and knowledge on the part of its maker, thus providing evidence of a certain level of intelligence amongst early humans. There has, however, been a great deal of debate as to what these often rather beautiful tools were actually used for. Suggestions range from digging tools to projectile weapons for big game hunting, thrown in a similar way to a discus. The fact that Aechuelian handaxes have often been found mixed up with the bones of large animals such as rhinoceros and elephant does reveal that they were used as heavy-duty butchery tools for dismembering and cutting meat. Nevertheless, it seems unlikely that they did not have other functions, and perhaps we would be better seeing the Acheulian handaxe as an all-purpose tool, the Lower Palaeolithic equivalent of the Swiss Army Knife!

We leave aside the Old Stone Age and turn to the Mesolithic (or 'Middle Stone Age'). This period was much shorter lived than the Palaeolithic, and archaeologists normally place its beginnings around 10,000 BC at the end of the last Ice Age. Steven Mithen (a leading expert on prehistoric hunter-gatherers) has pointed out that although the archaeological boundaries between the Palaeolithic and Mesolithic are somewhat blurred because people led similar lives during these periods, the Mesolithic was nevertheless 'a period of significant cultural achievement in the spheres of technology, subsistence, and art'.

Like their counterparts elsewhere in Britain, the hunter-gatherer communities of Wales would have led a somewhat nomadic existence, their lives dictated by the wild food sources that they could glean from land and sea. Often, all we have to attest to their elusive lives are flint tools or 'lithics' found lying in the landscape. However, although these communities would have been highly mobile, archaeology has revealed that in the Mesolithic at least, some of their settlements seem to have been of a permanent nature. One such settlement was located at Howick on the Northumbrian coast near Bamburgh, where archaeologists have recently discovered what appear to be the remains of a Mesolithic roundhouse built around 10,000 years ago. The house is likely to have had a pitched roof, which probably covered in thatch or turf and supported by strong wooden posts. The remains of a central hearth containing grey seal, wild pig, bird, and fox bones was discovered inside the house, along with masses of hazelnut shells that had been discarded around the hearth. It appears that the house was in use for some 150 years, and it is quite possible that the various people who lived in it throughout the years were members of an enduring Mesolithic family. By a strange archaeological coincidence, a similar Early Mesolithic house (around 10,000 BP) was discovered some forty miles north of Howick at East Barns in East Lothian, at the same time as the Northumbrian site was being excavated.

Another Mesolithic house was also recently found at the famous site of Starr Carr, North Yorkshire. It was constructed between 9200 and 8500 BC, and, as yet, is the oldest house to have been discovered in Britain. Although this circular, post-built dwelling was not particularly large (3.5 metres in diameter), the large posts (about 20 cm in diameter) used in its construction are seen as evidence of a substantial and sophisticated structure that was probably permanent in nature. Inside the house, its occupants laid a floor of organic material (perhaps moss and reeds) in a purpose-built hollow measuring 2.5 metres long, and the presence of burnt flints found here indicate that the house also had a hearth. What materials were used to cover the walls and roof of the house is unknown, but reeds or turf may well have been used, or alternatively, animal hides.

Across the Irish Sea, in County Derry, there is the fascinating site of Mount Sandel. Here, on a bluff that overlooked the River Bann, Peter Woodman worked from 1973 to 1977 on the excavation of a Mesolithic settlement, uncovering much fascinating evidence about the lives of Irish hunter-gatherer groups. The settlement was built around 7000 BC. People here had lived in circular, dome-like dwellings with central hearths, which appear to have been constructed using bent saplings that must have been covered with hides, or other materials that have long since decayed. There may have been as many as ten of these fairly substantial structures (they were about 6 metres across, with some of the saplings measuring 20 cm in diameter), although they were not all occupied at the same time. The people who had lived at Mount Sandel had not gone hungry, as they lived well on a range of resources that included salmon, seabass, eels, hazelnuts, and wild pig. The animal remains found at Mount Sandel suggested that Mesolithic people may well have been living at the site right throughout the year, and it is possible that it was occupied by many different groups for several hundred years before it was abandoned. As David Miles (formerly Chief Archaeologist at English Heritage) says of this British and Irish Mesolithic evidence:

> These places show that Mesolithic hunters were not simply mobile nomads living in temporary shelters or tents [and that] where conditions were favourable they either lived in permanent sites or created places which could be visited regularly at appropriate times of the year.

Whether similar settlements also existed in the British Upper Palaeolithic has not been confirmed, but it would be very surprising if there were none at all, considering that the people of this time lived a very similar lifestyle to their Mesolithic successors. In fact, archaeological discoveries made elsewhere in Europe caution us against totally dismissing the idea that there were at least some settlements of a more permanent nature in Upper Palaeolithic Britain. Amongst the most remarkable of these discoveries were the remains of substantial, circular houses made largely from mammoth bones found at sites in central and eastern Europe (e.g. Dolní Věstonice in Moravia and Mezhirich, Ukraine). Mammoth bones were also used as structural components in some of the circular stone huts that have been found at large cave and rock-shelter sites in France (e.g. at the Grotte du Renne cave at Arcy-sur-Cure in central France). At Vigne-Brune in the Loire Valley, several different dwellings were found, and it seems likely that these represent a single settlement that was occupied at the same time by several different families. Similar settlements are suspected at other French sites such as Laugerie Haute, Abri Pataud and La Madeleine in southern France.

Whatever the truth is regarding the true nature of Upper Palaeolithic settlement in Britain, there can be no doubting that the arrival of modern humans in Britain during the Early Upper Palaeolithic (*c.*43,000–35,000 BC) was of huge significance – just as it was elsewhere in Europe. As the Palaeolithic archaeologist Paul Mellars has said:

> Over this period we can identify two major developments which, in one form or another, were clearly fundamental to the whole of the subsequent development of European society. On the one hand, this period witnessed the effective replacement (in the very broad sense of the word) of the earlier 'archaic' or Neanderthal populations of Europe by populations which are ... apparently identical to ourselves. And ... we can identify a wide range of changes in the archaeological records of human behaviour which collectively define the transition from the Middle to the Upper Palaeolithic periods.

The many innovations that emerged in the Early Upper Palaeolithic have led several archaeologists to talk of a 'creative explosion' in the Early Upper Palaeolithic. This is nowhere more vividly demonstrated than in the impressive and hauntingly beautiful paintings that Upper Palaeolithic people left in caves such as Lascaux in southern France, or Altimira in northern Spain. In addition to the cave paintings there are numerous smaller, but equally beautiful, objects carved from bone, antler and ivory. One of the most remarkable of these is the lion-headed human figure made from mammoth ivory, which was found at the Vogelherd cave in southern Germany. Thousands of personal decorative items in the form of various beads and pendants, in most cases consisting simply of perforated teeth from species such as fox, bear and wolf, have also been recovered from numerous Upper Paleolithic sites. More elaborate ivory ornaments were made as well, and notable examples include the perforated beads possibly decorated to resemble seashells, which were found at La Souquette rock shelter in south-west France.

On a more practical level, Upper Palaeolithic communities also produced a much wider and diverse range of stone tools, which indicates that the communities of this time were more complex and sophisticated than the more conservative Neanderthal ones they replaced. This greater complexity and sophistication also seems to be reflected in the fact that at many Upper Palaeolithic sites the animal bones belong mainly to a single species (e.g. reindeer or steppe bison), and furthermore, many Upper Palaeolithic settlements on the continent were located in river valleys, along which game animals would have seasonally migrated. Such evidence points to a more specialised exploitation of animals by modern humans than that practised by the Neanderthals – although when it came to hunting, as we will see in the next chapter, the Neanderthals were not the 'dumb brutes' they are often cracked up to be.

It is hardly surprising that Wales' hunter-gatherers have left us with very fragmentary and elusive traces of their lives. Not only would the majority of their settlements have been very ephemeral in nature, but as mentioned earlier, people would also have been very thin on the ground in the Palaeolithic and Mesolithic, with total populations numbering in the thousands. Severe climatic changes have also played their part in obscuring our view of their remote and mysterious world, as the people of Palaeolithic Wales lived during the Pleistocene epoch (which is currently dated from around 1.8 million to 10,000 years ago), or 'Ice Age' as it is more commonly known. During this time, massive ice sheets and freezing conditions discouraged human settlement, although animal species such as woolly mammoth, brown bear, Arctic fox, and woolly rhino roamed the landscape.

However, as Nick Barton (Professor of Palaeolithic Archaeology at Oxford) has noted, the term 'Ice Age' is something of a misnomer, as during this lengthy chapter in the human story there were actually many separate cold and warm phases, rather than one single 'big freeze', with glaciers repeatedly advancing and retreating (evidence pertaining to many Palaeolithic communities must have been wiped out because of this process). In fact, during one of these warm, or 'interglacial' phases (cold phases are unsurprisingly known as 'glacials') dating from around 127,000–117,000 years ago, summers were warm (with temperatures around 73°F on average), winters were mild, and archaeology has shown that early humans would have been able to hunt elephants, rhinos, and hippopotami (the remains of a hippo from this period were discovered underneath Trafalgar Square). However, if present evidence is telling us the true story, then it seems that the animals did not have to fear hunters, as there were no humans living in Britain at this time. It should also be pointed out that we are actually living in an interglacial phase at present, and, at some point, the ice will come again. As Neil Oliver says in his highly readable book *A History of Ancient Britain*, 'The uncomfortable truth is that we are presently enjoying one of [these] summer holidays from the ice – and have been for the last 11,500 years or so'.

Thanks to an important scientific breakthrough, whereby it is possible to date the ancient sediments found on ocean floors, we now know that there have been eight Ice Ages, and that the extreme glacial and interglacial periods were relatively short-lived. More than half of the Ice Ages were also actually something of a mixture of both glacial and interglacial periods, with environments that changed from scattered woodland conditions to succeeding bare but unglaciated tundra landscapes.

The 'end' of the Ice Age, and the subsequent melting of the glaciers which had covered large swathes of Europe, also undoubtedly played a part in wiping out evidence for Welsh hunter-gatherers. Many low-lying areas were lost to the sea because the subsequent rise in sea-levels turned Britain into an island, with the last land bridges linking it to the continent finally disappearing beneath the waves around 8,000 years ago in the later Mesolithic (many Early Neolithic sites were also lost because this post-glacial rise in sea-level reached its maximum some 6,000 years ago). During the Mesolithic in Europe, the open tundra landscapes of the Upper Palaeolithic were replaced by thickly carpeted dense forests, with oak, pine, willow and birch, amongst other tree species, spreading throughout the continent. In contrast with the Upper Paleolithic, a much greater range of animals also lived amongst the Mesolithic landscapes of Europe, and its seas were also more richly populated, providing Mesolithic communities with more opportunities for food. However, many of the large mammal species of the Upper Paleolithic, such as woolly rhino, Mammoth and giant deer, did become extinct in the Mesolithic.

It was not just glacial meltwaters that have robbed of us of evidence of Britain's hunter-gatherer communities, as around 6100 BC a tsunami wreaked havoc along the eastern seaboard of Britain. It was caused by the collapse of a seabed shelf (measuring over 200 miles long) about 70 miles off the coast of Norway, which pushed a huge wave (30 feet high) towards Britain. Neil Oliver has said in regard to this monstrous wall of water: 'People and animals in its path would have been obliterated, smashed to smithereens. All that had been there before, all but the bedrock, was washed clean away'. It is also known that this Mesolithic tsunami penetrated as far as 50 miles inland.

Remarkable evidence pertaining to these drowned hunter-gatherer sites (and people) comes from 'Doggerland', which is an area of land roughly equivalent to the size of England. This post-glacial region would once have been a rich hunting ground for both Late Upper Palaeolithic and Mesolithic hunter-gatherers, until it was finally drowned beneath the waters of what is now the North Sea. The remains of tree stumps and fallen trees that can be found around many parts of the Welsh coast also provide a fragile and fascinating testimony to the landscapes that disappeared as a result of the rise in sea levels at the end of the last Ice Age. They perhaps also provide us with a pertinent reminder of the dangers that we face because of current global warming. Although there are a few later examples dating to the Bronze and Iron Ages, most of these 'submerged forests' (as they are known) date to the Late Mesolithic and Early Neolithic (c.7000–3500 BC) and can be found at low tide on several beaches right around the Welsh coast (the one found at Borth Sands, Ynyslas, Ceredigion, is particularly impressive). The submerged forests have been the subject of scientific and archaeological research for over 200 years, but it was the twelfth-century churchman, Giraldus Cambrensis (also known as 'Gerald of Wales', 'Gerald the Welshman', or *Gerallt Gymro*), who appears to have first recorded their existence in 1188 in his fascinating medieval travelogue *The Journey through Wales*. This fascinating figure of the Middle Ages, who was descended from Norman Marcher Barons and Welsh princes, tells us of his crossing of Newgale Sands on the coast of Pembrokeshire, after a fierce storm:

> Tree-trunks became visible, standing in the sea, with their tops lopped off, and the cuts made by the axes as clear as if they had been felled only yesterday. The soil was pitch-black, and the wood of the tree-trunks shone like ebony ... the sea-shore took on the appearance of a forest grove, cut down at the time of the Flood, or perhaps a little later.

Archaeologists have uncovered several strands of evidence relating to the lives of Mesolithic hunter-gatherers at several of the Welsh submerged forests, and unsurprisingly, Mesolithic stone tools have been found at several of these (e.g. at Lydstep Haven, Amroth, and Freshwater West in Pembrokeshire). Whilst I was writing this book, I was lucky enough to find a possible flint tool close to the Carreg y Defaid submerged forest, which is located on the Warren beach just outside Abersoch in Llŷn. A few weeks later, I also found a large piece of flint on Porth Neigwl beach. Gwynedd Archaeological Trust have examined it and told me it is very unusual to find such a large piece of flint this far north in Wales. Thus there is a chance that it may have been imported by human hands at some point during the prehistoric period. However, it is also possible that it was transported by glacial action, or it may even have once been used as ship's ballast!

Other remnants of Mesolithic life have also been found at the submerged forests, such as the antler mattocks from Rhyl and Uskmouth. The remains of what appears to have

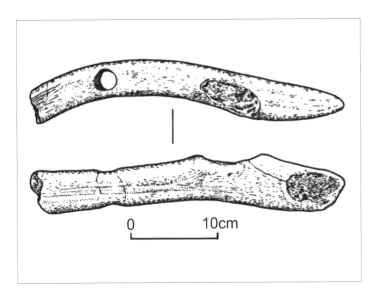

Antler mattock from Rhyl
(Redrawn after Bell et al)

been a temporary Mesolithic shelter and hearth were reported by J. P. Gordon-Williams in the early twentieth century, at the Frainslake submerged forest in Pembrokeshire. He says in regard to this discovery: 'Here a wind-screen of gorse, birch, hazel, and I think, alder was set in the peat'; he also tells us that a large area of charcoal and several flint tools were found on the north side of this shelter.

It appears likely that the submerged forests which lie off the coast of Ceredigion gave rise to the famous Welsh tale of Cantre'r Gwaelod ('the lowland/bottom hundred') that tells of the drowned medieval kingdom of the ruler Gwyddno Garanhir (*garanhir*: longshanks – *garan*: heron, *hir*: long) which now lies beneath Cardigan Bay:

Beneath the wave-swept ocean
Are many pretty towns
That hearkened to the bell-rings
Set pealing through the night
Through negligent abandon
By a watcher on the wall
The bells of Cantre'r Gwaelod
Submerged beneath the wave.

*Translated by Dyfed Lloyd Evans
from the original poem, 'Clychau Cantre'r Gwaelod'
by J. J. Williams*

There are several versions of the tale, although the negligent watcher is often named as the drunkard Seithennin, who, one stormy night, after enjoying himself rather too much at the spring feast held at Gwyddno's Llys (court) in Aberystwyth, forgot to shut the huge gates that were built into the great dyke, which defended Cantre'r Gwaelod from the sea.

No doubt, the long parallel ridges or *Sarnau* that can be seen jutting out to sea below the waters of Cardigan Bay also played a part in fostering the legend of Cantre'r Gwaelod. Although the Sarnau do look man-made, these are actually accumulations of banks of rounded pebbles and boulders (Boulder Clay) that were deposited as a result of glacial action. The largest, Sarn Badrig (*'Patrick's Causeway'*), extends some eleven miles into the Bay from the Mochras peninsula. Intriguingly, though, William Owen Pughe (a Welsh antiquarian and prolific author) did claim to have seen large slabs lying in a heap on the sea bed, about four miles out from the coast, during a sailing trip on a calm summer's day in the summer of 1770. He attributed these to 'the remains of the fort of Gwyddno'. However, as F. J.

North points out, considering that Pughe did not write about this trip until some sixty years later, it seems more probable that what he had actually seen were the larger than average boulders lying at the seaward end of Sarn Gynfelyn.

Whatever the truth is about Cantre'r Gwaelod, despite the problems that we are faced with when it comes to trying to piece together the lost world the Welsh hunter-gatherers, there have been several discoveries that – if only for a little way – allow us to travel back into this deeply fascinating world.

Julian Heath
Liverpool
Spring 2013

Chapter 1

Neanderthals on the Edge of Europe

Anybody who has visited the Elwy Valley in Denbighshire will understand why the poet, Gerald Manley Hopkins, was moved to write the words:

> Lovely the woods, waters, meadows, coombes, vales,
> All the air things wear that build this world of Wales.

from 'In the Valley of the Elwy', *1918*

However, many visitors to this enchanting corner of north Wales may not be aware that it is also the location of a site of international archaeological significance – Pontnewydd Cave. The cave lies about 6 miles to the north-west of Denbigh in the parish of Cefn Meiriadog on the western edge of the Vale of Clwyd, and is located in one of the steep limestone outcrops that rise dramatically above the Afon Elwy on the eastern side of the valley. Today, only the exterior of the cave can be visited; its interior is now necessarily protected by stone walling and a stout, securely-locked iron door. However, a visit to this site is still thoroughly recommended, as you will be able to stand in a place where early humans once stood, and, as a bonus, you will experience what is surely some of the loveliest countryside in Britain.

During the nineteenth century, the geologists Professors William Boyd Dawkins and T. H. McKenny Hughes (who was assisted by the Reverend D. R. Thomas, the vicar of the nearby village of Cefn at the time) successively investigated the site, recovering bones from animals now extinct in Britain (such as hippopotamus and rhinoceros), flint artefacts, and significantly, a very large human molar tooth which appeared to be as old as the animal bones. Although this tooth has unfortunately since been lost, the realisation that it was apparently as old as the animal bones raised the exciting possibility that there were further early human remains to be found in the cave. This possibility has since been turned into fact, thanks to the renowned Paleolithic scholar, Stephen Aldhouse-Green. He directed a series of meticulous excavations at the cave for the National Museum of Wales (*Amgueddfa Cymru*) from 1978 to 1995, and in the process, he uncovered hugely important evidence pertaining to early Neanderthal activity on the far north-western fringes of Europe about 225,000–175,000 years ago.

As well as further bones belonging to extinct Ice Age animals (e.g. bear, wolf, leopard, horse, bison, and lion), the excavations produced hundreds of stone tools, among which were numerous handaxes and scrapers, as well as many sharp flakes and blades. The handaxes, flakes, and blades may well have been used together as the component parts of a butchery kit, whilst the scrapers would probably have been used in the cleaning and preparation of hides, which were put to various uses: for example, clothing and bedding. Could it perhaps even be possible that animal hides were stretched over wooden frameworks by Neanderthals to make boats similar to the traditional coracles still used in parts of Wales today? This may be unlikely, but it is not impossible.

It does seem probable, though, that boats made from animal skins were made in the Mesolithic at least, as what appeared to be a paddle was found during Graham Clark's excavations (1949–1951) at the famous site of Starr Carr in Yorkshire. Clark argued that as there would not have been

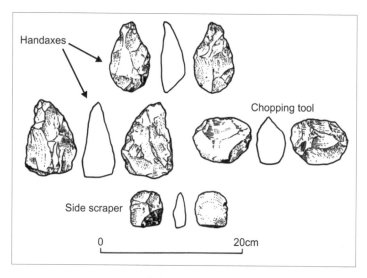

Stone tools from Pontnewydd Cave
(Redrawn after Green)

any trees in the locality big enough to make Mesolithic log boats, then the paddle must have come from a skin boat. It should be pointed out that a few log boats probably dating to the Mesolithic have been found in Scotland and Ireland. If Mesolithic people made boats – as seems likely – then it is also quite possible that their Upper Palaeolithic predecessors did too.

Several small, stone points were also recovered from the cave and these may have been used as the tips of hunting spears or javelins.

Many of the stone tools found at Pontnewydd Cave were made using the 'Levallois technique', of which more will be said below. Analysis of the stone tools revealed that a variety of different rock types had been used in their production, all of which would have been available locally. Burnt stones were also recovered during the excavations, and it seems likely that these indicate the use of fires for warmth, cooking (and maybe also protection) by the cave's occupants. It is also not hard to see why early Neanderthals chose to live in the elevated cave, as aside from providing obvious shelter from the harsh climate that existed at the time, it would also have provided a very good vantage point for spotting any game that passed through the valley below.

Somewhat amazingly, actual physical evidence of some of these occupants was also recovered, as fragmentary human remains also came to light during the excavations: an upper jaw fragment with a worn milk tooth and molar in place (this has been dated to about 225,000 years ago), belonging to a child aged about twelve years old; a vertebra; and some twenty teeth from at least five individuals – maybe even as many as fifteen. Many of them were probably males, around twenty years old. The most interesting aspect of this scanty skeletal material, however, is that some of the molar teeth clearly show the 'taurodontism' (enlarged pulp-cavities and coalesced roots), characteristically seen in Neanderthals. Some scholars would view such evidence as being indicative of the existence of 'pre-Neanderthal groups' rather than actual 'early' Neanderthal ones in the Elwy Valley. However, at the least, as Stephen Aldhouse-Green and Elizabeth Walker have said:

> It is probable that the Pontnewydd People were at an early stage of the evolutionary process which produced the fully developed Neanderthals who lived from about 70,000–30,000 years ago.

Whatever label one prefers for the 'Pontnewydd people', how their remains ended up in the cave remains something of a mystery. Nonetheless, like Stephen-Aldhouse Green, I feel that it is unlikely that they were dragged into the cave by carnivores and more probable that they represent the remains of people who were deliberately buried in the cave by mourning families.

In this respect, it might be interesting to mention here that at the site of Atapuerca in northern Spain, the remains of over thirty individuals who had died around the same time as the Pontnewydd Neanderthals were found in a small chamber set deep within a complex of caves. Although it not clear whether they arrived here by design or chance, as we will briefly see below, there is strong evidence to be found which suggests that formal burial (sometimes with grave goods) was not as uncommon amongst the Neanderthals as some archaeologists like to propose.

It is hard to say with absolute certainty what the Elwy Valley looked like at the time of the Pontnewydd Neanderthals, but it may have been an open steppe-like environment, as they lived at the cave in the middle of an interglacial period (about 245,000–30,000 years ago) when the climate was probably deteriorating, with much colder

Location of Coygan Cave before its destruction
(Carmarthenshie County Museum)

conditions than we are used to. One thing is for certain though – it would have been very different from the beautiful and idyllic place that made such an impression on Gerald Manley Hopkins some 100 years ago.

Coygan Cave

Sadly, Coygan Cave has now been obliterated by quarrying operations, but it was located at about 60 metres above our present sea level on Coygan Rock, an outcrop of Carboniferous Limestone situated between Pendine and

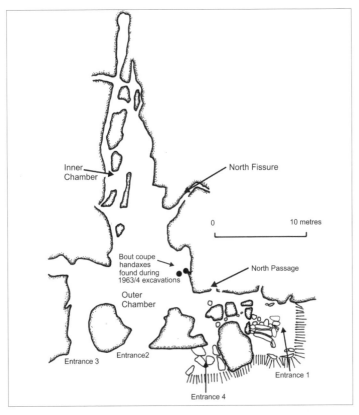

Plan of Coygan Cave
(Redrawn after Aldhouse-Green et al)

Laugharne in Carmarthenshire (*Sir Caerfyrddin*). Before its destruction the cave was a popular draw for fossil-hunters, and various archaeological investigations were also carried out intermittently at the cave in both the nineteenth and twentieth centuries. Along with numerous bones belonging to Ice Age animals – for instance, mammoth, woolly rhino, bison, cave lion, and spotted hyena (the majority of the bones came from the latter species, revealing that Coygan Cave had been a hyena den) a small collection of stone tools were also recovered from the cave. The most significant artefacts amongst the lithic assemblage were three *bout coupé* handaxes. One of these was found by Herbert Eccles,

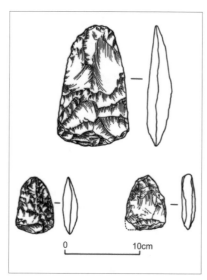

who dug at the cave in 1913 and 1914, and the other two came to light during the last excavations at the cave, which were carried out by the University of Cambridge in 1963 and 1964 under the direction of Professor C. B. M. McBurney and Mr J. Clegg. The three handaxes were all made from a flint-like chert material. As Joyce Tyldesley (who is better known as a prolific and respected author of

Bout coupé *handaxes from Coygan*
(Redrawn after Aldhouse-Green et al)

books on Ancient Egypt) has rightly remarked, two of them are surprisingly small, although as she further notes, this may be because there was a limited supply of raw material for handaxe manufacture. The *bout coupé* handaxes revealed

Excavations in progress at Coygan, 1913
(Carmarthen County Museum)

that 'classic' Neanderthals had occupied the cave, and although it is generally felt that it is more likely that this occupation took place around 50,000 years ago, there is a chance that Neanderthals were actually living at the cave some 12,000 years later. Further evidence of the Neanderthal occupation of the cave is probably provided by the remains of a hearth, which McBurney reported as finding 5–10 metres inside the cave.

If Neanderthals were indeed living at Goygan Cave as late as *c*.38,000 BP, then it could perhaps even be possible that they were sharing the Welsh (or at least the wider British) landscape, with modern human groups of the Early Upper Palaeolithic. It may even be the case – as Stephen Aldhouse-Green and Elizabeth Walker have suggested – that the Coygan Neanderthals could have been pushed to a site in the far west of Britain because incoming Early Upper Palaeolithic groups of modern humans displaced Neanderthals from their favoured areas of settlement in Europe. It is an interesting theory, and one which is perhaps supported by the fact that not only are *bout coupé* handaxes very rare in Wales (fewer than ten have been found) but also, the majority of *bout coupé* handaxes have been found in low-lying river valley sites in southern and eastern England.

As we saw in the introduction, the human jawbone found at Kent's Cavern near Torquay appears to indicate that modern humans were present in Britain at least as early as 41,000 BP. Although not all archaeologists may agree on this date, the fact that archaeological evidence found elsewhere in Europe suggests that the beginning of the Upper Palaeolithic dates to *c*.43,000–40,000 BP, then it becomes more feasible. We have no modern human remains from Wales dating to the beginning of the Upper Palaeolithic, but several archaeologists believe that the distinctive Upper Palaeolithic 'Leaf Points' found at several sites in Wales, and elsewhere in Britain, date back to as early as 38,000 BP.

Joyce Tyldesley tells us in her important study of *bout coupé* handaxes that translated from French into English, *bout coupé* literally means 'cut-tip', although several

British archaeologists have interpreted it as 'cut-butt'. Some archaeologists prefer to refer to *bout coupé* handaxes as 'flat-butted cordate', or 'flat-based cordiform' handaxes, and strictly speaking, it would be more correct to do so, but the French name does have a nicer ring to it. Although not they are not that common, *bout coupé* handaxes form a striking and rather elegant part of the 'Mousterian' industry,

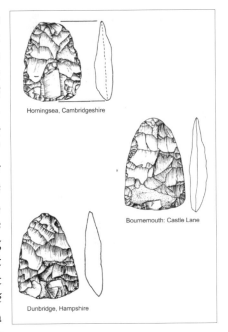

Horningsea, Cambridgeshire

Bournemouth: Castle Lane

Dunbridge, Hampshire

Bout coupé *handaxes from England*
(Joyce Tyldesley)

which is a distinctive tool-making tradition almost exclusively associated with the Neanderthal people of Western Europe; although it is evident that Mousterian-type tools were made by some modern human communities in the Near East and Africa during the Early Upper Palaeolithic. (The 'Mousterian industry' takes its name from the site of Le Moustier in south-western France, where there are two rock-shelters that were occupied by Neanderthals around 45,000 years ago.)

Archaeologists are somewhat in the dark when it comes to the question of what *bout coupé* handaxes were actually used for. Their size and shape strongly imply that these impressive artefacts were hand-held tools of some sort. But because of the general wear and tear that the majority have suffered over the millennia, and because they are often covered with a thick white patina, their edges are not particularly suitable for microwear analysis. It is quite possible that they were mainly used as butchery tools. Several of the *bout coupé* handaxes recovered from sites in England (such as Woolpack Farm, Cambridgeshire, and Johnson's Pit, Kent) were found in association with the bones of animals such as mammoth, woolly rhino, horse, reindeer and red deer. However, whilst such evidence does strongly does point towards their use in butchery, perhaps it is more likely that rather than having one specific function, *bout coupé* handaxes were actually multi-functional tools that had a variety of uses. Joyce Tyldesley has also noted that not only are *bout coupé* handaxes usually found as isolated finds, but if they were ordinary everyday tools, then it appears that more work than was strictly necessary often went into the production of these elegant artefacts. Of course, this does not prove that bout coupé handaxes were never used as tools, but as Tyldesley has asked: 'Could it be that the extra work involved in their manufacture gave them some prestige or ceremonial value beyond their actual functional worth?'

A brief look at the Neanderthals

The Neanderthals first emerged from the darkness in which they had lain hidden for many thousands of years when a partial human skeleton was discovered in the Feldhofer Cave in the Neander Valley (near Düsseldorf) in 1856. Since then, the Neanderthals have been of great interest to scientist and layman alike, and no doubt this will continue to be the case. As the archaeologist Paul Pettit has rightly pointed out, our deep fascination with the Neanderthals can be put down to the fact that they are the only other type of human species to have shared the earth with us. To earlier archaeologists and anthropologists the Neanderthals were little more than semi-simian savages of low intelligence, and although this image still exists to some extent in the popular imagination, archaeology has shown that it is far from the truth. Nick Barton has pointed out that:

> in recent years, this image has been transformed by new excavations and analyses which show Neanderthals as fellow human beings with sophisticated tool-making skills and a complex social organisation.

While *bout coupé* handaxes such as those found at Coygan Cave clearly demonstrate the great skills that Neanderthal craftsmen possessed (and their probable appreciation of beauty), they are not are as common as the side-scrapers, denticulates, backed knives, and notches that were also made by them. Microwear studies have shown that these implements were used in butchery, the preparation of animal hides and for making other tools and artefacts out of organic material such as wood or antler. Microwear analysis has also revealed that small triangular stone points found at Neanderthal sites were once inserted into wooden spearshafts that have long since decayed, and in fact, at the site of Umm el Tlel in the Syrian Desert (which dates to *c*.50,000 BP) a broken spear point was found in the neck of a wild ass. Remarkably, evidence of how the Neanderthals helped to fix their stone tools securely into wooden shafts was recovered in 1963 from a lignite mine in the foothills of the Harz Mountains in Germany. Two pieces of birch-bark pitch were found in a layer dating to around 80,000 BP in a mining pit, and one bore a fingerprint along with the impressions of a flint blade and wood-cell structures. Thus as German archaeologist Johann Koller and his colleagues have rightly remarked, this piece of pitch had quite obviously been used as an adhesive by a Neanderthal to fix a flint knifeblade into a wooden handle.

It is evident that Neanderthals hunted 'big game', as shown by the 120,000-year-old yew lance found in an elephant carcass discovered at the Neanderthal site at Lehringen in Germany. Archaeological discoveries have also shown that Neanderthals were quite sophisticated hunters, and one of the most interesting and dramatic sites in this regard is La Cotte de St Brelade on Jersey. Here, mammoth and woolly rhino bones were discovered with Neanderthal stone tools in two piles in Middle Palaeolithic levels dating to about 180,000 years ago, at the foot of a 30 metre-deep ravine at the end of a headland. This evidence points strongly towards organised hunting parties, with Neanderthals driving panicked herds across the headland to the ravine which was literally a death trap. However, leading palaeoanthropologists Christopher Stringer and Clive Gamble have argued that the evidence found at Neanderthal sites shows that big-game hunting was not the norm, and that they preferred to hunt smaller and less dangerous animals such as reindeer, red deer and horse. Some of the healed injuries that are frequently seen on Neanderthal skeletons probably occurred through hunting, when Neanderthals ran down their prey to attack it at close quarters. In fact, in his analysis of injuries seen on Neanderthal bones, Neanderthal expert Erik Trinkaus has found some interesting comparisons with the injuries suffered by modern rodeo riders – suggesting that sometimes Neanderthals hunted at very close quarters indeed! However, it may also be possible that some injuries were received during violent conflicts that may have been more frequent amongst Neanderthal communities or individuals than we may like to think.

Although rare, remarkable discoveries such as the one

made at the Romani rock-shelter near Barcelona remind us that time must have robbed us of countless items of Neanderthal material culture that were made of perishable materials. At this site, excavators have recently discovered several flat and elliptical pieces of wood that had been abandoned beside the remains of one of the hearths discovered here. These objects had slight depressions in their centres, which has led the excavators – probably quite rightly – to assume that they were prehistoric platters on which food had been prepared and eaten. Interestingly, the platters were made of juniper, which is a wood that is quite resistant to fire and less likely to warp when being used near the heat of one. Two wooden implements found in the rock-shelter were probably used as digging sticks, and cavities found near the hearths contained wood fragments, perhaps indicating that this was where the Romani Neanderthals had stockpiled the wood that fed the fires which lit and heated the shelter. It seems likely that as well as providing heat and light in the rock-shelter, these fires were also used to cook on, and the natural fossil casts or 'pseudomorphs' of three logs that were found right on top of one of the hearths may indicate the presence of a former tripod used for cooking. Another pseudomorph of a log was found near this hearth, suggesting perhaps a fireside seat for the Neanderthals who had lived in the rock-shelter.

Another distinctive feature of Neanderthal culture is their common use of the 'Levallois' technique to produce their stone tools, which we have already briefly come across at Pontnewydd Cave. The technique takes its name from the Paris suburb where it was first recognised by archaeologists in the nineteenth century. It marks an important change in the way early humans made stone tools. Previously, they had left it to chance when striking suitable flakes for tools from stone cores, but with the introduction of the Levallois technique, the size and shape of these flakes were being predetermined by careful preparation of the core beforehand. It is not exactly clear when and how the Levallois technique appeared in Europe, but as Nick Barton tells us, some experts have proposed that this innovation in stone tool technology first appeared in Africa around 300,000–250,000 years ago, and from there spread into Europe via the hominid species *Homo helmei*, which they regard as the Neanderthal's most recent common ancestor. However, as he further notes, other experts feel that a 'proto-Levallois' existed in Europe in the Lower Palaeolithic period as early as 420,000 years ago, and that the later Levallois technique developed from this. Whatever the reality is, using the Levallois technique required intelligence and skill, and the Neanderthals became particularly adept in using it to produce fine stone tools. As Paleolithic scholar Brian Hayden says:

> even today, there are few students of lithic technology that can achieve a Neandertal's [*sic*] level of expertise in producing good Levallois cores or flakes, while the number of contemporary flintknappers that have successfully mastered the technique for producing good Levallois points probably number less than a score.

Nick Barton has remarked that, while we can never know whether Neanderthals had religious or spiritual beliefs, the discovery of deliberate Neanderthal burials strongly indicates that they 'developed emotional attachments to individuals within their society'. Those archaeologists who sit in the 'anti-burial' camp argue instead that either natural processes account for Neanderthal burials, or at best, the dead were disposed of in hastily dug pits or simply covered over with earth, basically being viewed as little more than domestic waste. However, as Barton has further said: 'Such views are almost certainly wrong, because they fail to take into account all of the available evidence'. Amongst this evidence is that discovered at La Ferrassie in France where two adults and five young Neanderthal children seem to have been deliberately laid out in a cemetery of small pits. Furthermore, one of the child burials had been covered with a limestone block that had been engraved with eighteen small cup-like depressions and the pits containing the two adults appear to have deliberately been positioned so that their occupants lay head to head in death.

In central France, there is the famous adult Neanderthal skeleton known as the 'Old Man of La Chapelle', found at La Chapelle-aux-Saints in a purposely dug flat-bottomed and straight-sided pit. The skeleton (which dates to c.60,000 BP) was also possibly accompanied by grave goods in the form of stone tools and bovid bones. Around 70,000 years ago, far to the east of these burials, at the cave of Teshik Tash in Uzbekistan, a Neanderthal community buried the partial skeleton of a child and then drove the horn cores of mountain goats into the ground around the child's burial. Of course, as Clive Gamble has argued, it could be rather than representing some burial rite, the horn cores were placed around the burial to protect it from scavengers. If this was the case, they proved ineffective in this respect, as the bones of the child were gnawed by animals. However, even if the horn cores were intended as a deterrent, it still suggests that the child was loved and cared for by the people responsible for the burial, as they did not want the remains desecrated.

No matter how brief, no account of Neanderthal burials can fail to mention the famous Neanderthal 'flower burial' discovered at Shanidar Cave in the Zagros Mountains of northern Iraq. During fieldwork carried out at this famous and fascinating site between 1951 and 1960, the American archaeologist Ralph S. Solecki discovered the remains of at least eight Neanderthals' skeletons (several of which showed signs of severe trauma) ranging in age from very young infants to 'old' men ('Shanidar 3' had lived to about fifty years of age – very old for a Neanderthal). They had been buried in the cave at different times between about 65,000 and 35,000 years ago. During the last season's work at the cave, Solecki took soil samples from within and around the area where one of the adult skeletons had been buried (Shanidar IV – an adult male), which were later analysed by the French palaeobotanist, Arlette Leroi-Gourhan. She discovered pollen from at least eight species of flowers and concluded from her analysis of it that Shanidar IV was laid to rest 'on a bed of woody branches and flowers … sometime between the end of May and the beginning of June'. Alternatively, it may be that garlands of flowers were actually strewn across the corpse after it had been placed in the grave. Ralph Solecki has eloquently said of this discovery: 'With the finding of flowers in association with Neanderthals, we are brought suddenly to the realization that the universality of mankind and the love of beauty go beyond the boundary of our own species. No longer can we deny the early men the full range of human emotions'.

It should be pointed out, however, out that some archaeologists have argued – perhaps somewhat unconvincingly – that the 'flower burial' at Shanidar Cave is a fallacy, and that instead, the pollen was probably introduced into the cave by the Persian *jird* (a small, gerbil-like creature which is known to live in burrows in caves), or alternatively, was introduced into the grave by workers on the excavations, or simply blown in from the outside.

Another contentious issue amongst Palaeolithic experts is whether Neanderthals produced 'art', but again, it can be argued that the evidence is stacked against the sceptics. We have already seen an example of Neanderthal 'art' above, with the cup-marks carved on the limestone block at La Ferraisse, but several others can be cited. For example, a piece of flint from the Israeli site of Quneitra dating to around 54,000 years ago features four carefully-engraved semi-circles and other lines, while at Riparo Tagliente in Italy similarly engraved flint flakes and pebbles have been discovered, one of which has a double arc incised on it.

The cup-marked limestone block at La Ferraisse was not the only Neanderthal 'artwork' to be discovered at the site, as one of the Neanderthal burials discovered here contained a small bone that featured a series of fine, carefully-incised marks, and at the site of La Quina in the Charente region of France, archaeologists discovered a bovid shoulder blade that had been incised with very fine long parallel lines. At the Bulgarian cave of Bacho Kiro, some 47,000 years ago, a Neanderthal left behind a bone fragment onto which he or she had engraved a zigzag motif. In fact, the sites of La Ferraisse, La Quina, and Bachro Kiro are a just a few of the many Neanderthal sites where deliberately engraved animal bones have been found. Several small, decorated objects that can not be assigned any utilitarian purpose have also been found at Neanderthal sites: for example, from Axlor in Spain there is a circular sandstone pebble featuring two cup-marks and a central groove, and from Tata in Hungary, we have an elongated and finely polished plaque

Fossil nummulite with cross motif from Tata, Hungary
(Author)

made from part of a mammoth molar. Also found at Tata was the fossil 'nummulite' (single-celled marine organisms with disc-like shells) that features an interesting cross-like motif on both sides, which was formed from a combination of a natural fracture and engraved lines.

One of the most fascinating Neanderthal portable art objects yet recovered comes from the cave of La Roche-Cotard in Indre-et-Loitre. An excavation was undertaken at the cave in 1975, and along with stone tools, archaeologists unearthed a worked piece of flint with a natural tubular perforation, through which a bone splinter was jammed. This highly intriguing piece has been plausibly interpreted by the French archaeologists, Jean-Claude Marquet and Michel Lorblanchet, as a 'proto-figurine' which was intended to represents either a human or animal face (perhaps a big cat). It is also evident that the Neanderthals were not averse to wearing 'jewellery', as evidenced by such finds as the reindeer phalange with a hole bored through its top, and the partly-finished pendant made from a fox tooth, which were also found at the previously-mentioned site of La Quina. Furthermore, there is the rich collection of personal ornaments found at the Grotte du Renne cave at Arcy-sur-Cure (Yonne), which included a bone fragment with a carved hole, and pendants made not only from fox and wolf canines, but from fossil shells also. The Neanderthals also liked to collect objects that could have had no practical function: objects such sea-shells of non-edible species, as well of lumps of iron pyrites, manganese dioxide, and ochre. The latter were often used in burials such as that of the 'Old Man' of La Chapple, who appears to have had ochre sprinkled around his head when he was laid to rest. At the cave of Pech de l'Azé (Dordogne) over 200 blocks of manganese dioxide and twenty-three of iron oxide were recovered, and many seem to have been worn down

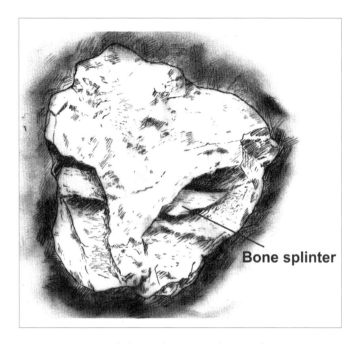

Bone splinter

Worked stone from La-Roche Cotard,
possibly representing a human or animal face
(Author)

into a 'crayon' shape through their repeated use on a soft surface of some sort.

Undoubtedly, one of the most mysterious aspects of Neanderthal life is how they communicated with each other: did they have complex language like us, or is it more probable that their language was 'simple in construction and restricted in its range of expression', as Christopher Stringer and Clive Gamble feel? Neanderthal experts are sharply divided as to the answer to this question and it seems unlikely that its answer will ever be fully resolved. Evidence that Neanderthals had similar vocal skills to modern humans may perhaps be provided by the almost complete Neanderthal skeleton found in a grave dating to about 60,000 BP at Kebara Cave on Mount Carmel in Israel. A hyoid bone very similar to a modern human one had also survived as part of the skeleton, and in modern humans, the hyoid bone is closely linked to the vocal tract. This has thus led some experts to argue that the Kebara hyoid bone shows that the Neanderthals possessed similar vocal skills to us. However, others have counter-argued that as pigs also possess similar hyoid bones to modern humans, then the one found at Kebara provides no proof whatsoever of this. The debate about the sophistication of Neanderthal speech will doubtless rumble on, but perhaps Brian Hayden is right with his assertion that 'there is no compelling reason to believe that Neanderthal language was fundamentally less complex than fully sapient language, although it may not have been *as* developed and probably had a different grammar'.

Perhaps the greatest puzzle posed by the Neanderthals, though, is how, after surviving for around 220,000 years, they came to disappear from the face of the earth, leaving us as the sole surviving species of the genus *Homo*. Modern humans are often seen as the culprits when it comes to the great mystery that surrounds Neanderthal extinction, and the popular perception is that the Neanderthals were wiped out by modern human groups as they spread out across Europe and other areas of Neanderthal habitation during the Early Upper Palaeolithic. The reality, however, is more complex. Archaeology has shown that not only did Neanderthal and modern human populations live alongside each other in some regions (e.g. Siberia), but furthermore they sometimes got *very* close to each other indeed, as has been revealed by a remarkable discovery made in 1998 at the Lagar Velho rockshelter in central western Portugal. At this site, archaeologists discovered that a young child (probably a boy) aged about four had been buried in a shallow but clearly cut grave, the edge of which was lined with stones and bones. The boy's skeleton was largely complete and was associated with a pierced periwinkle shell which he had probably worn as a pendant, and he had also been covered with red ochre by the people who had buried him. Those responsible for his burial had also placed a red deer coccyx and the spine of a rabbit in the grave, and radiocarbon dates obtained on the latter showed that he had died between 25,000 and 24,000 years ago in the Upper Palaeolithic. The nature of his burial suggests that the boy may well have been an important member of his community, but as Frances Pryor says in his excellent book *Britain BC*: 'The real interest in the Lagar Velho boy lies in the anatomical form of his bones, which are clearly those of *Homo sapiens*, but also reveal a number of distinctively, and very strongly marked Neanderthal features'. As it seems to be the case that actual Neanderthals had died out in this region some 6,000 years before the burial of the Lagar Velho boy, then the discovery of surviving Neanderthal traits in his skeleton indicates that the first modern human groups who colonised this region must have interbred with its original Neanderthal populations on a regular basis

Today, the general consensus among the experts is that Neanderthals were not wiped out in some prehistoric 'blitzkrieg' by invading hordes of early modern humans, but rather, they were gradually forced into more marginal areas and eventual extinction by more 'advanced' early modern humans who ultimately outdid them in the struggle for survival. However, although I do not particularly want to end this chapter on a pessimistic note, it seems likely that in some parts at least, there is a more sinister explanation behind the disappearance of the Neanderthals. Paul Pettit has said in this regard:

> It must have seemed, in some areas, that Neanderthals had little to offer modern humans – except competition.

In these areas, the attitude may have been to kill first, ask questions later. For too long we have regarded the extinction of the Neanderthals as a chance historical accident. Rather, where Neanderthals and modern humans could not coexist, their disappearance may have been the result of the modern human race's first campaign of genocide.

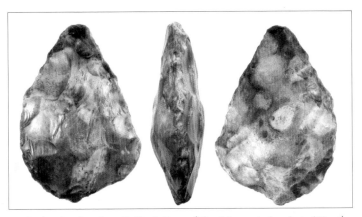

Acheulian handaxe from Cadfarch, Powys (Clwyd-Powys Archaeological Trust)

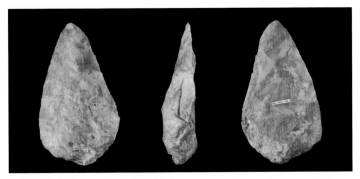

Aecheulian handaxe from Alergia (Creative Commons, Didier Descouens)

Possible prehistoric Abersoch)

Possible prehistoric stone tool found near Carreg y Defaid submerged forest, Abersoch (Author)

*Carreg y Defaid submerged forest near Abersoch
(Author)*

0   5cm

Mesolithic blade from Gwynedd (Gwynedd Archaeological Trust)

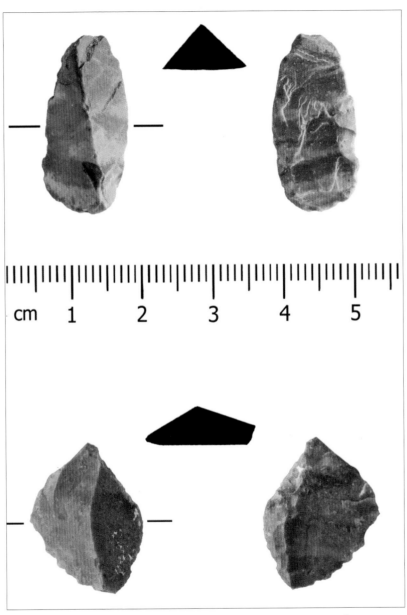

Mesolithic lithics from Flintshire (Clywd-Powys Archaeological Trust)

Exterior of Pontnewydd Cave (Author)

Ffynnon Beuno (Eirian Evans)

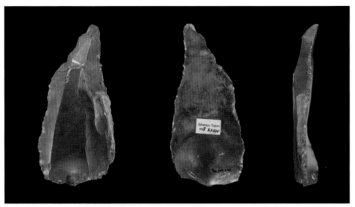

Levallois blade from The Valley of the Kings, Egypt
(Creative Commons, Didier Descouens)

Levallois flake Andelys, France (Creative Commons, Didier Descouens)

Location of Pontnewydd Cave (Author)

Replica of a bout coupe handaxe
made by Joyce Tyldesley
(Joyce Tyldesley)

The Elwy Valley (Author)

Goat's Hole, Paviland (Chris Elphick)

Aveline's Hole (Rod Ward)

Long Hole Cave (Rod Ward)

Neolithic tomb, Parc le Breos Cwm (Dai Barnaby)

Cathole Cave (Chris Elphick)

Cathole Cave (Dai Barnaby)

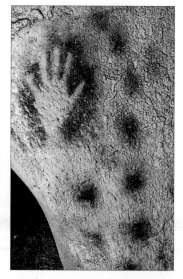

Hand stencil, Pech Merle Cave, France (PD-Art)

Ice Age Engraving of Bison from Cresswell Crags (Paul Bahn)

*Painted pebble from Le Mas-d'Azil
(Creative Commons, Didier Descouens)*

*The Venus of Willendorf, Austria
(Creative Commons,
Don Hitchcock)*

Paintings of horses in Chauvet Cave (PD-Art)

*Upper Palaeolitic artists at work in Font-de-Gaume Cave, France
(Charles R. Knight PD-Art)*

Aerial view of Waun Fignen Felen (RCAHMW)

*Excavations at St James' Street Monouth
(Steve Clarke, Monmouth Archaeology)*

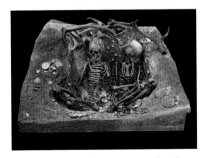

*Mesolithic bural containing two females,
Teviec, Brittany
(Creative Commons, Didier Descouens)*

*Mesolithic Microlith (Creative
Commons, Jose-Manuel Beniti)*

The Afon Lledr Creative Commons, Noel Walley)

The Brecon Beacons (Adrian Pingstone)

Looking towards The Nab Head from above Musselwick Sands (Deborah Tilley)

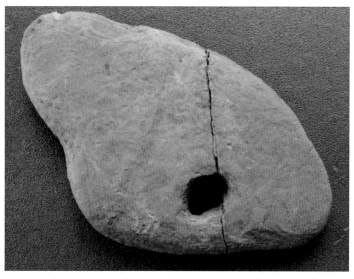

Perforated mudstone bead found at the Trefael stone (George Nash)

*Catrin Murphy standing next to Mesolithic footprints on Lydstep Beach
(Dyfed Archaeological Trust)*

Stones marking positions of Mesolithic posts

Bryn Celli Ddu Passage Grave (Martin J Powell)

Pen Cilan Head (Author)

Porth Ceriad and Trwyn yr Wylfa (Author)

Llyn Brenig (Stephen McKay) A

Medieval Hafod, Llyn Brenig (Author)

Monuments 51 & 8 at Llyn Brenig (Author)

Chapter 2

The 'Red Lady' in the Cave

Moving now from the mysterious Neanderthal inhabitants of Wales to the modern humans of the Upper Palaeolithic – who are no less intriguing – we arrive first at the Gower peninsula in south Wales.

The Gower is justly famed for its stunning beauty, but it is also a place of archaeological renown, as it was in Paviland (or Goat's Hole Cave), which lies just east of Port Enyon on the south coast of Gower, that one of the most remarkable prehistoric burials in British archaeology was discovered – the 'Red Lady' of Paviland. Numerous prehistoric burials have survived the ravages of time, all of them telling us something of the distant past, but some are more significant than others; the burial of the Red Lady is particularly significant.

The Discovery of the 'Red Lady'

The story of the Red Lady begins in 1822, when Daniel Davies, the Gower's first medical practitioner, and the Reverend John Davies explored Goat's Hole and found animal bones and a mammoth tusk. John Davies made further visits to the cave, and made further discoveries, including prehistoric stone and bone tools, and two Roman coins, which he gave to the Talbots of Penrice Castle to put in their family museum. As a result of this donation, Miss Mary Theresa Talbot, who like her mother (Lady Mary Cole) and sister (Miss Jane Harriot Talbot), was interested in natural history and geology, became aware of the exciting archaeological potential of the cave. It is thus hardly surprising that she accompanied Lewis Weston Dillwyn (a family friend who had published works on natural history and botany, and encouraged the Talbot family in their studies) on two expeditions to explore the cave in December 1822. Their explorations met with success, as they discovered many mammoth bones and teeth, which also found their way into the Talbot family museum.

Subsequently, Dillwyn and Lady Cole contacted William Buckland, who was the first Reader of Geology at Oxford (and later Dean of Westminster), to let him know of the discoveries made at Goat's Hole. By 18 January 1823, Buckland had arrived in Gower, and within a week he found the burial of the Red Lady, which undoubtedly ranks amongst the most famous discoveries in British archaeology. Buckland describes the find in his grandly titled *Reliquiae Diluvianae; or, Observations on the Organic Remains Contained in Caves, Fissures, and Diluvial Gravel, and on Other Geological Phenomena, Attesting the Action of an Universal Deluge* (1823):

> [the skeleton] was enveloped by a coating of a kind of ruddle ... which stained the earth, and in some parts extended itself to the distance of about half an inch around the surface of the bones ... Close to that part of the thigh bone where the pocket is usually worn ... [were] about two handfuls of small shells [which were perforated] of the *Nerita littoralis* [periwinkle shells] ... At another part of the skeleton, viz in contact with the ribs [were] forty or fifty fragments of ivory rods ... from one to four inches in length ... [also] ... some small fragments of rings made of the same ivory and found with the rods ... Both rods and rings, as well as the Nerite shells, were stained superficially with red, and lay in the same red substance that enveloped the bones.

It should be noted that Buckland found a skeleton that lacked not only its skull, but most of its right side. What happened to the skull is unknown, but it is quite possible that it was deliberately excluded from the burial, and deposited elsewhere, or perhaps even curated as a focus of ancestor worship. On the other hand, it may simply be the case that it was carried away by the sea with the rest of the missing bones, as the sea is known to have broken into the cave at times in the past. Today, these skeletal remains are kept in the Museum of Natural History in London, although we might perhaps wonder whether they should be repatriated to the National Museum of Wales.

The red ochre (Buckland's 'ruddle') found on the bones shows that the Red Lady went to the grave wearing ochre-stained clothing, and the distribution of this ochre on the skeleton suggests that the clothing may have consisted of a two-piece garment and shoes. Many archaeologists feel that red ochre was symbolic of blood and the human life force (as it is today in some cultures), and speculate that perhaps prehistoric people believed that by covering the dead in it they were 'reanimating' them for the journey to the Otherworld.

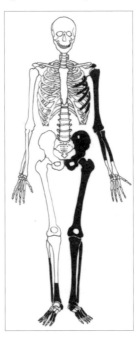

Skeleton of the 'Red Lady'
(Redrawn after Wallis)

I should also mention the remains of a large mammoth skull that Buckland found close to the head of the Red Lady's grave during his excavations. How it had ended up in Goat's Hole is unclear, but it is perhaps possible that the mammoth had entered here to die, although if the topography of the cave was similar to that of the present, then it must have been a very agile mammoth! Alternatively, and perhaps more plausibly, the skull was transported to the cave by the people responsible for the burial. Why they may have gone to the effort of moving what would have been a very heavy object will be discussed later.

In addition to the mammoth skull, Buckland, and the various individuals who subsequently investigated Paviland Cave after his work at the site, recovered many hundreds of animal bones from other extinct animal species. Some of the bones can no doubt be related to the presence of human groups at the cave, but it also appears likely that human use of the cave was interspersed with periods of occupation by carnivorous animals. The most common species represented in the bone assemblage were horse, woolly rhinoceros, reindeer, bison and bear; also present were giant deer, mammoth, wolf and hyena,

As Stephen Aldhouse-Green and Paul Petitt have pointed out, the title of Buckland's *Reliquiae Diluvianae* ('evidence of the flood') reminds us that at this stage of his career he believed in the literal truth of the story of Noah and the great flood recorded in Genesis, chapters 6–8. Thus he put forward the theory that the extinct animal bones had arrived in Goat's Hole both by being washed in by the Biblical flood, and by animals falling in through the aperture in its roof. Buckland also postulated that these two processes accounted for the appearance of extinct animal bones found in other British caves. The fact that the burial of the Red Lady was found in close association with extinct animal bones and prehistoric flint tools was of little consequence to Buckland's interpretation of the burial. To be fair to him though, he did not have the battery of sophisticated dating methods that are available to modern archaeologists. Also, as Marianne Sommer has pointed out, although scientists were beginning to glean the true antiquity of mankind around the time of the discovery of the Red Lady, its story was still largely influenced by the chronology of the Bible. In his later career, Buckland did reject his earlier Flood theory, readily accepting that a much longer chronology lay behind the human story. Although Buckland made many more visits to Gower after his remarkable discovery, he never returned to Goat's Hole to undertake further investigations at the site.

There were further archaeological discoveries in the other Paviland Caves – Hound's Hole Cave and Foxhole Cave. Hound's Hole was also excavated by Buckland and later by Odo Vivian, but although horse, deer and bear bones were found, no lithics were recovered. However, Stephen Aldhouse-Green and his team did discover a possible Early Upper Palaeolithic blade at Hound's Hole, during the most recent excavation at the Paviland Caves in 1997.

Prior to 1997, Foxhole Cave had never been archaeologically investigated, and the excavations here proved to be more productive than at Hound's Hole. The animal remains included reindeer, horse, and collared lemming dating to

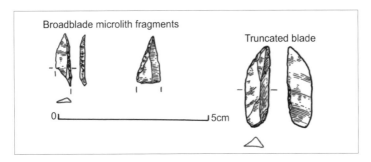

Early Mesolithic stone tools from Foxhole Cave
(Redrawn after Wallis)

the Late Upper Paleolithic. Also found were several Early Mesolithic stone tools, a human tooth from a Mesolithic individual, and a possible hearth dating to either the Late Upper Palaeolithic or the Early Mesolithic.

Further evidence of Upper Palaeolithic hunter-gatherers was found at Long Hole cave, which is located at the top of sea cliffs that lie about a mile to the east of the Paviland Caves. The cave was first investigated by Colonel E. R. Wood in 1861 and later re-examined by John Campbell who uncovered a three-metre thick deposit that probably dates back to around 125,000 years ago. Amongst the finds from the cave were a small collection of Upper Palaeolithic tools along with a worked bone point which may possibly have been made by Neanderthals in the Middle Palaeolithic. Also found were bones belonging to extinct animals such as bear, wolf, reindeer, mammoth, straight-tusked elephant and narrow-nosed rhinoceros.

Buckland's Interpretation of the Red Lady

From a letter written by Buckland to Lady Cole, shortly after the discovery of the Red Lady, we learn that he and his co-workers at the cave had originally decided that the skeleton belonged to that of an exciseman who had been murdered and deposited in the cave by smugglers, who were notorious along this stretch of the Welsh coast. However, the letter also reveals that Buckland then changed his mind and decided that the bones in fact belonged to a witch, rather than a customs officer. He decided this on the basis that the well-travelled Giraldus Cambrensis wrote about the use of mutton bones in divination in *The Journey through Wales*. In fact, it was not the native Welsh who Gerald recorded as practising this strange custom, but rather, Flemings (Flemish) who were settled in Pembrokeshire (far from peacefully it should be said) by the Anglo-Norman

King Henry I in around 1108. He tells us that by examining the right shoulder-blades of rams which had been boiled and stripped of meat, the Flemings could 'foretell the future and reveal the secret of events long past'.

John Traherne (an amateur geologist), who, along with Dillwyn and Miss Talbot, had accompanied Buckland to Goat's Hole and other caves in the vicinity, saw the letter that Buckland had written to Lady Cole and subsequently wrote his own letter to Buckland informing him of the existence of an ancient fort on the clifftop immediately above Paviland Cave. This letter made Buckland offer up his final suggestion as to the occupation of the Red Lady, and, although – as Nick Barton has pointed out – we do not know whether Buckland was making some elaborate pun (he was well known for his eccentric sense of humour and love of practical jokes), in her final transformation, she literally became a 'scarlet woman', or prostitute, who ensured the Roman soldiers in the above fort did not 'get lonely' in this remote outpost on the far edge of the empire. Buckland, however, was firing well wide of the mark with his somewhat racy interpretation of the Red Lady, as not only is the fort Iron Age in date, but 'she' was actually a 'he', and the burial was made many thousands of years before the Romans ever set foot in Wales.

An Early Upper Palaeolithic Burial

The dating of the Red Lady to the Roman period was not challenged until 1911, when Emile Cartailhac, an eminent French prehistorian, examined the evidence from Goat's Hole at Oxford, and concluded that the Red Lady was actually laid to rest in the 'Aurignacian', a sub-division of the Early Upper Palaeolithic (42,000–30,000 BP). Cartailhac was supported in his conclusion by another notable French prehistoric scholar, Edouard Lartet, and by Henry Christy, a

London banker and industrialist, who was also a keen ethnologist, archaeologist and collector of antiquities.

As a consequence of this renewed interest in the Red Lady, because collectors were continuing to turn up finds from Goat's Hole, and because scholars were beginning to get a firmer grasp of Palaeolithic chronology, Professor William Sollas (a successor of Buckland at Oxford) decided that the time was right to return to the cave to undertake new excavations. Thus in the summer of 1912, Sollas spent several weeks digging the cave with his team, which included the Abbé Henri Breuil, a Catholic priest who was also a leading authority on Palaeolithic cave-art.

Sollas made many new and important discoveries shedding further invaluable light on prehistoric activity in the cave, including limestone boulders located where the foot and head of the grave of the Red Lady would have been. Not unreasonably, Sollas says of these boulders: 'It seems, therefore, extremely likely that that boulders had been placed in position – one at the feet and two at the head of the corpse – at the time of the internment'. Whether these were actual gravestones deliberately set up by the mourners at the Red Lady's funeral is debatable, and, as Sollas himself admits, it is a little odd that Buckland made no reference to these.

On the other hand, as Stephen Aldhouse-Green has remarked, these limestone boulders '[are] out of character in terms of size with the uniformly small limestone scree which filled the cave'. Sollas also found around 600 flint tools during his investigations at the cave, and these form part of a lithic assemblage that contains over 5,000 items (this assemblage ranges in date from c.40,000–11,000 BP, with the earliest lithics perhaps indicating the presence of Neanderthals at the cave), though his most intriguing find was the ivory egg-shaped pendant (known as the 'Sollas

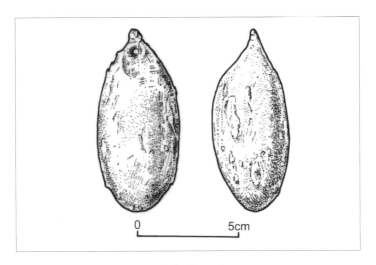

The 'Sollas egg'
(Redrawn after Wallis)

egg') that was made using a growth from the injured tusk of a mammoth. The latter was actually uncovered by Buckland during his work at the cave nearly ninety years earlier, and it was Sollas who proved that the two were one and the same by taking the pendant to Oxford, where the tusk was kept. As he says in his excavation report: 'We were therefore able to compare them, and found that they tallied to a nicety, the egg-shaped body fitting into the cavity of the injured tusk'. Sollas made the interesting suggestion that 'Magic powers were probably attributed to so rare and remarkable an object and it might have been suspended in the cave or slung round the neck of the hunter to bring him good luck'.

Whilst the pendant is obviously Palaeolithic in date (it has been dated to around 24,000 BP, although it could possibly be much older), it was not found in association with the burial of the Red Lady. As mentioned previously, Buckland found around fifty fragments of cylindrical, ivory rods in contact with the ribs of the Red Lady, and Sollas also

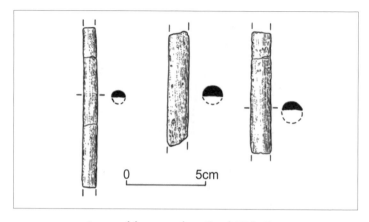

Ivory rod fragments from Goat's Hole Cave
(Redrawn after Wallis)

came across several similar fragments in the vicinity of the burial. The possible significance of these highly intriguing artefacts will be discussed below. In addition to these artefacts, Sollas also discovered two human bones (the end of a humerus (arm bone) and a first metatarsal bone from a foot) in Goat's Hole, but these date to the Mesolithic and probably represent a burial made at the site around 7,200 BP.

Amongst the most fascinating Upper Palaeolithic artefacts to have been recovered from the cave are the unique 'spatulae' made from horse and deer bone, which were unearthed by collectors during the 1830s. Two of these were found by Colonel George Grant Francis and John Gwyn Jeffreys in 1836, who left evidence of one of their visits to the cave with a graffito on its roof, which reads 'CGF + JGJ + 1835'. They also discovered Roman coins and pottery, as well as bones belonging to an infant. Unfortunately, however, the whereabouts of the latter are unknown and thus we cannot say at what date the child was buried in the cave. The Reverend John Davies found a third spatula at the cave in around 1939–40, and it seems likely that all three spatulae were deposited together in the cave at the same time. Nobody truly knows what these enigmatic objects were used for, but Stephen Aldhouse-Green has argued that they can be compared with similar artefacts found at Upper Palaeolithic sites in Moravia and Russia, which are probably highly stylised representations of the female form (these similarities perhaps hint at very far-flung exchange networks in Upper Palaeolithic Europe). It is quite possible, if not likely, that these eastern European spatulae had some sort of religious significance, and it seems probable that the same can be said for their Welsh counterparts. As

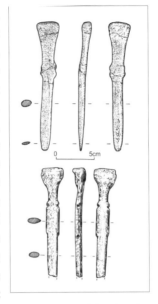

Bone 'spatulae' found with the 'Red Lady'
(Redrawn after Wallis)

Francis Pryor has said in regard to this idea, the Paviland spatulae display exceptional craftsmanship, and the fact that the three appear to have been deliberately deposited together suggests that they had a 'special', rather than an 'everyday' purpose.

Sollas and Buckland also found several pieces of worked ivory (some of them ochre-stained) in the form of plate fragments and modified lumps during their excavations. Although the purpose of the former is something of a puzzle, the lumps of ivory could plausibly have been used as *lissoirs* or burnishers on animal skins, in order to make them tougher, more waterproof, and generally more pleasing to the eye.

The exact date of the Red Lady's burial will never be known for certain, but the most recent – and more reliable – dating programme carried out in 2007 by Roger Jacobi and Thomas Higham on two of the Red Lady's bones indicated that the burial probably took place around 33,000 years ago. The previous dating programme on the skeleton of the Red Lady, which was undertaken in the late 1990s, came out with a date of c.26,000 BP for the burial and thus the new dating programme appears to show that it is considerably earlier than was previously thought. The programme also pushed back the date of the spatulae from the previously accepted 23,000 to 26,000 BP, and it is even possible that they are considerably older than this; Jacobi and Higham have said that '[they] prefer to regard this as a minimum age' for these artefacts. They have also argued that the previous dates obtained for the 'Sollas egg' and the worked lump of ivory of unknown purpose should not be seen as reliable. However, they were unable to redate these two objects, and thereby could not support their argument that these were also much older than previously thought.

In his report of the 1912 excavations Sollas also provided a detailed examination of the bones of the Red Lady and he suggested that 'she' was in fact, a 'tall' and slender young man (about 5 feet 8 ins), aged between 20–25 years. Modern analysis of the bones lends strong support to this suggestion, but one young man probably died in his mid, rather than his early twenties. This analysis has also revealed that he enjoyed a diet that also included fish; these may have been caught on the coast (which was then 100 km away from Goat's Hole) during the seasonal movements of his community, or alternatively, fished from the nearby 'palaeo-Severn' river.

William Buckland made no serious attempt to examine the bones of the Red Lady, and he simply assumed that the skeleton was female on the basis of the ivory rings, or bracelets, which were also found with the burial. His thoughts in this respect are revealed in a later paper which he gave to the British Archaeological Association:

> There never was, nor ever will be, a period when, even among uncivilized races, the female part of our species were not, and will not be, anxious to decorate themselves with beads. They are at this time highly prized by the negroes of Africa, and the Indians of America.

Conveniently, Buckland seems to have forgotten that it was not only the women, but also the men of 'uncivilized races' who like to adorn themselves with bodily ornaments, and coincidentally, his statement also reveals the Victorians' attitude of moral superiority towards non-Europeans.

Although scholars such as Cartailhac and Sollas revealed that Buckland's interpretation of the Red Lady was a good story, and nothing more, it is only in recent years that we have come closer to an understanding of this remarkable individual from the remote past, and the intriguing place where he was buried. This is thanks largely to Stephen Aldhouse-Green, who was instrumental in the modern reassessment of the evidence from Goat's Hole and edited what he called *Paviland Cave and the 'Red Lady': A Definitive Report* (see bibliography for publication details). Given the new dates obtained by Jacobi and Higham, he was probably a little unwise in his use of 'definitive' in the title, but the report nevertheless contains a wealth of fascinating information on this hugely important and fascinating site, and it seems unlikely to be bettered.

An Upper Palaeolithic Shaman?

The Red Lady appears to have been an important person who was deemed worthy of a special burial. Although we can only obviously only speculate as to how this young man had gained his status, one possibility worth considering in this respect is that he was an Upper Palaeolithic shaman (a healer, or 'medicine man'; one who was considered to be in touch with the spirit world) who was revered (and maybe also feared) by his community. That this may have been the case could be indicated by the evidence found in association with the burial, and perhaps it is the ivory rod fragments that point most strongly in this direction. As Stephen-Aldhouse Green has noted, although it is possible that these rods were blanks for the manufacture of beads, they show no evidence that they had been prepared with this function in mind. He has therefore suggested that it could be that they were 'magical wands' used in religious rituals and ceremonies. Such an interpretation may seem somewhat fanciful, but as Aldhouse-Green further remarks, Sollas documented one fragment in his report, which may lend further support to this idea. Sollas tells us: 'Mr H. Balfour found one fragment in Miss Talbot's collection with one end preserved: it is slightly swollen and well rounded off'. It might also be worth bearing in mind that there are many instances in the ethnographic record of shamans (who are commonly found in hunter-gatherer societies) using rods and staffs as 'tools of their trade'. Interestingly, as Francis Pryor has mentioned, the San hunter-gatherers of the Kalahari Desert in southern Africa, used ochre-painted rods very similar to those found with the Red Lady, in their religious ceremonies. In their fascinating book, *The Quest for the Shaman*, it has also been suggested by Stephen Aldhouse-Green and his wife Miranda (a renowned authority on Iron Age and Romano-Celtic ritual and religion) that the perforated periwinkle shells found by Buckland on the thigh of the Red Lady may once have been held in, or decorated, a 'medicine bag'. As they have said: 'These shells speak not only of journeys to the coast, but perhaps also of journeys to the underwater world of the spirits'.

The large mammoth skull found close to the grave of the Red Lady perhaps also hints at the shamanic role that this young man played many thousands of years ago. It is well known that animals form a crucial part of shamanic belief systems and often, in hunter-gatherer communities, one particular animal (usually the one that the community depends upon for its survival) is perceived as an animal-helper that aids the shaman as he moves between the world of the living and the dead. Alternatively, it may perhaps even be possible that the mammoth skull was used as a percussive musical instrument, or 'osteophone', perhaps on the occasion of the Red Lady's burial. Soviet archaeologists have claimed that several mammoth bones painted with red ochre, which were found at the Upper Palaeolithic site of Mezin, near Kiev, were used by a prehistoric 'orchestra' and even recorded themselves playing these possible instruments in a jam session!

Another possibility in respect of Palaeolithic music-making is that the marvellous 'draperies' of folded calcite formations that are found in number of Upper Palaeolithic cave-sites, were used as 'lithophones', which were struck with hard wooden sticks to produce clear and resonant notes. Interestingly, in several caves on the continent, there are calcite formations that show clear signs of ancient damage, and some of them are also decorated with mysterious painted lines and dots – though I am not suggesting that they represent prehistoric musical notation!

Some readers may raise a scornful eyebrow at such suggestions as the above, but music-making was certainly not unknown in the Upper Palaeolithic, as evidenced by the discovery of over thirty bone flutes from various archaeological sites in Europe. These are made on bear, reindeer and bird bones, and are not unlike the penny whistles with which we are familiar. Several Upper Palaeolithic oval bone and ivory objects displaying a hole at one end have also been interpreted as possible examples of the 'bullroarers' (swung around the head like a lasso to produce a high-pitched, humming sound) used nowadays in rituals and ceremonies by various non-state societies such as the Australian Aborigines and the North American Indians.

It may be interesting to mention that there have been several richly furnished Upper Palaeolithic burials found in continental Europe, some of which bear similarities to that of the Red Lady, and these may also mark the final resting places of prehistoric shamans. A particularly interesting example of one such burial was found at Brno in Moravia. The burial was found far from any settlement site and contained the ochre-covered skeleton of a mature adult male (who had suffered greatly with chronic pain in his bones as a result of periostitis) lying underneath a mammoth scapula (shoulder blade). Mammoth tusks,

Ivory 'marionette' from Brno, Moravia (Author)

mammoth and woolly rhinoceros ribs, ochre-stained horse teeth, and a number of intriguing objects were found in the grave of this putative eastern European shaman. The latter included two large perforated slate discs, lumps of haematite, fourteen small discs made of stone, bone and ivory, a reindeer antler with a polished end that was perhaps a drumstick, and some 600 perforated sea shells. These latter artefacts may have come from a head-dress, and a remarkable, highly mysterious ivory figurine (known as the 'marionette') was also found with the burial.

A Place of Upper Palaeolithic Pilgrimage?

We can only guess as to why, many thousands of years ago, a Palaeolithic community chose to bury the Red Lady in such a striking location, but it is certainly possible that it was because the cave and/or hill were seen as sacred by Upper Palaeolithic communities. Even today, Goat's Hole Cave and its locale inspire awe in the adventurous modern visitor; it must have been even more so to the prehistoric one – though perhaps for different reasons. Stephen and Miranda Aldhouse-Green have said of this striking location:

> In prehistory – in an age of belief – it must truly have seemed to be a place of oneiric (dream-like) power where terrestrial humans could approach and even enter the very *mons sanctus*, the holy hill, and in the Stone Age darkness engage with the world of spirits.

As we will see in the next chapter, a rare and significant discovery may recently have been made in another Gower Cave not far from Goat's Hole, and this could provide further support for the idea that caves were spiritually special places for people of the Upper Palaeolithic.

Of course, this is not to deny that caves could also function on a practical level during this time, and there is evidence to suggest that Goat's Hole was used as place of temporary occupation by hunter-gatherers previous to the burial of the Red Lady. Stephen Aldhouse-Green has made the interesting suggestion that those responsible for this ceremonial burial were drawn to the cave because of the perceived presence of ancestral spirits. Furthermore, he has suggested that objects such as the 'Sollas egg' and the ivory spatulae deposited there reveal that it continued to be a special place thousands of years after the burial of the Red Lady, with Palaeolithic 'pilgrims' visiting this 'holy hill' (albeit sporadically) right down until around 21,000 BP, when Britain was locked in the icy grip of a full glacial period that peaked around 18,000 years ago.

However, this attractive idea has come under attack from various quarters, and Palaeolithic scholars Roger Jacobi and Thomas Higham are among its critics. They feel that the results of their dating programme do not support this hypothesis and have stated: 'Taken together, the evidence for human visits to Goat's Hole subsequent to the Red Lady burial is now hardly credible. Instead, the archaeology of the cave is now telling us a simpler story'. Jacobi and Higham argue that most of the artefacts found in Goat's Hole belong to a period of occupation that took place prior to the burial and that people did not subsequently visit the cave, ritually depositing such items as the mammoth pendant and bone spatulae (which they refer to as knives). Stephen Moss (who stayed overnight in the cave) is another detractor of those who feel that Goat's Hole was akin to a prehistoric church, in which a powerful shaman or leader was laid to rest. Writing recently in the *Guardian* he says:

> What might be called the Welsh romantic view of the Red Lady is given academic backing by a monograph called *Paviland Cave: A Definitive Report* ... Unfortunately for the definitive report, the skeleton had been wrongly dated to 26,000 years ago, and the case for the symbolic importance of the cave and its possible shamanic status of its occupant is now though distinctly sketchy.

Moss also tells us that Marianne Sommer has argued that Welsh academics have 'been seduced into making the Red Lady part of an indigenous cultural narrative', and that Tom Higham believes it is more likely that 'she' was probably buried in Goat's Hole after some sort of hunting accident. This is quite possible, but it could be argued that this theory is just as 'sketchy' – if not even more so – than Aldhouse-Green's, and personally, I feel he hits nearer the mark with his interpretation of the archaeological evidence found in Goat's Hole. True, the new dating programme may have pushed back both the date of the burial and the unusual ivory artefacts (or at least the date of the spatuale) found in the cave to an earlier time when the climate was warmer; thus dispelling the idea that even the extremely harsh conditions of a full glacial period could not keep people away from visiting this special place. However, it does not disprove the theory that – shaman or not – the Red Lady was a person of some status who was given the privilege of a ceremonial burial at a sacred site, which continued to be a focus of religious veneration long after he was laid to rest here. Perhaps though, this is just a romantic view, obscuring a more mundane truth about the young man from the Upper Palaeolithic, and the cave in which he was finally laid to rest?

Chapter 3

The Oldest Art in Wales

The decorated caves of the European Upper Palaeolithic undoubtedly provide us with some of the most remarkable and enigmatic testaments to prehistoric life. In these caves, which for the most part, are found in France and Spain, a wide range of animals (e.g. bison, mammoth, deer, bulls, lions, fish and birds) was depicted in both paintings and in

'The Polychrome Ceiling', Altamira, Spain
(P-D Art)

engravings on cave walls. Many of the paintings are stunning, and posses a powerful prehistoric beauty, but it is only a lucky few who have been able to view them in their natural settings. However, Werner Herzog's recent film *Cave of Forgotten Dreams* came close to providing this experience, with cinema-goers taken on a stunning 3D journey through the amazing Chauvet Cave in the Ardèche region of France (discovered in 1994, Chauvet Cave contains some of the most exquisite examples of Upper Palaeolithic cave art yet discovered). Along with the animals depicted in Palaeolithic cave art, there are paintings and engravings of both humans and 'humanoids' (that is, they cannot be positively identified as human), and composites or 'therianthropes' (figures showing both human and animal features). It is the depictions of animals, however, that are dominant. A wide range of non-figurative motifs or 'signs' (simple lines of painted dots and more complex grid-like patterns) are also found in abundance in the caves.

In addition to the cave (or *parietal*) art, Upper Palaeolithic communities in Europe also produced portable, or *mobiliary* art, which as the name suggests, would have been carried around by people. These objects were made from stone, bone, mammoth ivory, antler and amber (it seems likely that wood was also utilised), and came in many different forms, including beads, pendants, carved spear-throwers, carved figurines, and flat pieces of stone ('plaquettes') inscribed with images. As with parietal art, the many examples of portable art that have been discovered are decorated with images of animals, what appear to be human figures (these are more rarely seen), and abstract markings.

David Lewis-Williams notes in his fascinating book *The Mind in the Cave*, that some scholars of Upper Palaeolithic art have rightly pointed out that we must be wary of importing western connotations by uncritically using the word 'art'. However, as he further says:

> [although] the word has misled many researchers to understand Upper Palaeolithic imagery in terms of Western art ... I believe that we can become over-sensitive to this problem. 'Art is a handy monosyllable, and, provided we are aware of the dangers of its Western connotations, we can use it with caution.

The Cat Hole Cave Reindeer

While I was writing this book in 2011, news began to break of the discovery of Late Upper Palaeolithic rock art in Cat Hole Cave, which only lies some 10 kilometres to the east of Paviland Cave. If genuine, this is a find of considerable significance, as Upper Palaeolithic parietal art is extremely rare in Britain, although it is probable that as more detailed investigations are undertaken at other caves, more of this mysterious art will be discovered. The most notable examples of British parietal art yet found come from Church Hole Cave at Cresswell Crags in Nottinghamshire. In 2003, Paul Bahn and his colleagues discovered a series of remarkable engravings probably dating to some 13,000 years ago (there may be up to 90 images), which included fine depictions of a stag, a large bear and a bison, along with depictions of what may be a crane or bittern and a group of three geese. However, Paul Pettitt has made the alternative suggestion that these possible bird engravings actually represent highly stylised depictions of females similar to those seen in Upper Palaeolithic art from Germany. He has further suggested that they may represent women engaged in some sort of ritual dance, which could even have taken place inside the cave.

Another probable example of Late Upper Palaeolithic cave art has been found at Cheddar Gorge, Somerset, where what appears to be a crude drawing (also dating to about 13,000 BP) of a mammoth's head can be seen on a cave wall. In addition to the figurative engravings in Church Hole Cave, Bahn and his colleagues also identified non-figurative, abstract motifs. Similar engravings were also found in two other nearby caves (Robin Hood's Cave and Mother Grundy's Parlour). They feel that it is possible that at least one of the abstract engravings found in Robin Hood's Cave is sexually symbolic, and that it represents a vulva and part of the hips and waist of a female. Abstract prehistoric engravings (cross motifs and rectilinear designs) have also been found at the cave sites of Aveline's Hole (which was occupied during the Upper Palaeolithic but is best known as a rare Mesolithic cemetery where over fifty people were buried) and Long Hole in the Mendip Hills. Although it is possible that these engravings date to the Upper Palaeolithic, it is felt, on stylistic grounds, that they were probably produced during the Mesolithic.

Cat Hole Cave on the Gower is located in a striking rock outcrop in pleasant woodland at Parkwood, Parkmill, where there are several scheduled ancient monuments, including the well known Neolithic chambered cairn of Parc le Breos Cwm, and a relict medieval deer park. The cave was first 'excavated' in the 1860s, by Colonel E. R. Wood, who removed a large section of the cave floor, discovering several Upper Palaeolithic flint tools. The majority of the tools date to the Late Upper Palaeolithic, about 12,000 BP, although two possible 'Font Robert Points' were also found, perhaps indicating a much earlier human presence at the cave in the Early Upper Palaeolithic around 28,000 BP.

The bones of several extinct animals were also recovered by Wood from the same level as the Late Upper Palaeolithic flint tools, and among the species identified were wild cat, mammoth, hyena, bear, reindeer, elk, and possibly also cave lion and rhinoceros. The Colonel also discovered evidence of later prehistoric activity at the site in the form of Bronze Age pottery, a bronze axe, and human bones, probably from a burial or burials). Charles McBurney directed excavations of a more rigorous nature at the cave in the late 1950s, and around 300 flint tools were recovered. The majority of these date to the Late Upper Palaeolithic, although two 'tanged points' dating to c.28,000 BP were also found, indicating a human presence at the cave in the Early Upper Palaeolithic also.

Some fifty years later in September 2010, rock art expert George Nash and members of the Clifton Antiquarian Club visited Cat Hole Cave. They had had their interest initially piqued by the discovery of possible abstract engravings in the cave, during a visit made in 2007. (These are now considered to be more probably geological markings, although claw scratches made by cave bears were found.) In 2011 they were more fortunate and they discovered a possible engraving (measuring 15 x 11 cm) of what may be a stylised depiction of a reindeer in a discrete niche lying north-east of the main part of the cave. If it is indeed a human engraving, the 'reindeer' was probably engraved using a sharp, pointed flint tool. In style It resembles carved reindeer figures seen in Mesolithic rock art in Norway, although its location in a hidden corner of the cave is more typical of the Upper Palaeolithic.

Early in 2011, a team from the Open University visited the cave and took samples for Uranium Series dating from the surface on which the possible engraving was made, as well as a sample of later flowstone that covers the reindeer. A date of around 14,000 BP was obtained from the flowstone sample, and thus it seems that whoever had come into the cave to make the possible engraving had done so previous to this date. George Nash has said in this regard: 'My guess is that the reindeer is much earlier and could extend back as far as the Early Upper Palaeolithic, between 16,000

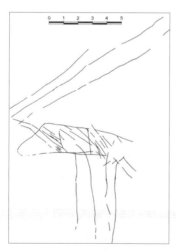

Tracing of 'reindeer' engraving from Cat Hole Cave
(George Nash)

and 30,000 years, at a time when the British climate was extremely hostile'.

However, as important a discovery as the Cat Hole 'reindeer' may be, a word of warning. Paul Bahn, a highly respected archaeologist and author, and a leading expert on European Ice Age art, has strongly argued that the Cat Hole 'reindeer' is very probably just natural cracks in the cave wall, and he feels that 'the press have muddied the waters' by reporting it as a genuine find. In the light of his argument, it is interesting to compare the tracing of the 'reindeer' made by Paul Brown (who recorded the Ice Age engravings in Cresswell Crags) with that made by George Nash and his colleagues. Unfortunately, though, the truth about the Cat Hole 'reindeer' will probably never be known, and it seems likely that opinion will remain sharply divided as to its authenticity.

No examples of painted cave art have been found in Britain, and because of our climate, it seems very unlikely that they ever will be. In 1912, at Bacon Hole in Gower, Professor William Sollas and the Abbé Henri Breuil did find ten wide bands of a reddish cave). They believed that they had a found a unique example of Palaeolithic painted cave art, but it was subsequently realised that the 'art' was simply red oxide mineral that had seeped through the cave wall.

Paul Brown's tracing of the Cat Hole 'reindeer'
(Paul Bahn)

The Meaning of Cave Art: Possibilities

Since scholars first began to pay serious attention to Palaeolithic cave art in the nineteenth century, various theories have been put forward as to what drove prehistoric people to make paintings and engravings in such places. Paul Bahn has noted in his excellent *Journey Through the Ice Age* (which includes many superb photographs by the late Jean Vertut) the earliest and simplest theory proposed by Palaeolithic scholars was that the cave art had no meaning and that it was simply 'art for art's sake', revealing the inherent desire that humans have to express themselves artistically. This view, however, has fallen out of favour, and there are very few – if at all any – scholars who now support it. However, this is not to deny that some Palaeolithic cave painters took some level of artistic pride in their work, even if, as seems likely, the paintings did have some deeper meaning.

Perhaps, also, the most talented of the cave artists were celebrated figures who acquired some level of status because of their skills. Of course, it is possible that the decoration seen on some portable objects is just that – decoration – and perhaps even some open-air engravings should be seen in the same light. However, it is very unlikely that the same can be said for the parietal art of the Upper Palaeolithic. As Bahn has rightly said in this regard:

> when parietal art began to be found, it rapidly became clear that something more was involved … the restricted range of species depicted, their frequent inaccessibility and their associations in caves … the enigmatic signs, the many figures which are purposely incomplete [or] ambiguous … and the caves which were decorated but apparently not inhabited all combine to suggest that there is complex meaning behind both the subject matter and the location of the Palaeolithic figures.

Hunting Magic and Totemism

In the early twentieth century, with the decline in the 'art for art's sake' explanation of Palaeolithic cave art, a new theory emerged to dominate cave art research. This largely came about as a result of anthropological research carried out amongst the Arunta people of Central Australia by Baldwin Spencer and F. J. Gillen, and by the work of Salomon Reinach (1852–1932), curator of the Musée des Antiquitiés at Saint-German-en-Laye, who was greatly influenced by Spencer and Gillen's account of the Arunta. Reinach argued that like the Arunta, people of the Upper Palaeolithic believed that the painting of certain animals on rocks would cause them to multiply, and thus provide more food. Similar 'sympathetic magic' can be seen elsewhere in the ancient world, and for example, the Egyptian elite carved and painted scenes of livestock and other food on their tomb walls in the belief that this would magically provide sustenance for the dead in the afterlife. Other Palaeolithic scholars such as the Abbé Henri Breuil and Henri Bégouën took up the hunting magic idea and ran with it, arguing that the cave art was produced by anxious Palaeolithic hunters who wished to ensure a successful hunt and that the missiles (spears and arrows) that appear to be depicted sticking into some animal (and human) images may have been painted to help to kill animals in the real world. Furthermore, it was argued that painted marks seen at the mouths or nostrils of animals represent dying animals, dots seen on their bodies were stones thrown at them, and that some of the abstract motifs represented throwing-sticks, arrows, lassos, and animal traps.

The hunting magic theory should not be totally ruled out, and perhaps in some cases we may have depictions of hunting. Yet this theory is not without its problems and inconsistencies. These have been highlighted by Paul Bahn.

For example, proponents of the theory argued that the scarcity of carnivores (e.g. lions or bears) in parietal art can be explained by the fact that these were dangerous animals that were difficult to hunt and which would not have made good eating. This is possible, but would not Palaeolithic artists have seen hunting magic as a very useful tool against dangerous animals, and thus painted them more frequently? Furthermore, it can be asked why reindeer and birds, which would have been important food resources to Upper Palaeolithic communities, are also rarely seen in parietal art. Some have argued that this was because there were plenty to go around; this seems to be a weak argument. Perhaps the missiles associated with some animal images provide the strongest support for the hunting magic theory, but it should be borne in mind that these images are not as commonly seen as we might expect, and it is not even certain that actual missiles are always being depicted.

Another theory about cave art, which was influenced by the research into the Australian Arunta, was that the animals depicted represented the emblems or totems of different clans or tribes. This idea, however, was not generally well-received, with its detractors arguing that if this was indeed the case, then several images of the same species would be expected, rather than images of different species. Nonetheless, the retort came back that this could reveal the different totems of several clans who formed one larger residential group. The argument continued back and forth, but it was soon superseded by the hunting magic theory.

One theory that has been popular in recent times is that cave art was made by Upper Palaeolithic shamans who entered caves in order to communicate with the spirit world. Some support (but not proof) that this may have been the case in the Upper Palaeolithic is provided by the fact that shamanism is commonly found amongst hunter-gatherer societies around the world. In these societies shamans were (and are) often the mediators between this world and the otherworld, and responsible for such things as curing the sick, ensuring good harvests, keeping evil spirits away, and so on. Often, the contact between the two worlds involved shamans being helped by spirit helpers, often in animal form, and shamans also commonly entered altered states of consciousness in order to travel to the spirit world – either through the use of hallucinogenic substances or other stimuli such as hypnotic chanting or drumming. In fact, it is perhaps possible that some of the composite human/animal figures that make rare appearances in cave art are actually depictions of Upper Paleolithic shamans. An interesting example in this respect is the strange 'Sorcerer' figure seen at Les Trois Frères cave in France, which has spreading antlers, a tail, paw-like upper arms, a tail, and an owl-like face. Interestingly, this figure is similar to an eighteenth-century depiction of a Siberian shaman. A half-human/half-bison figure is also depicted in the cave, and like the 'Sorcerer', this figure also seems to be engaged in some type of dance. It is worth bearing in mind, though, that these figures may actually be depictions of mythical beings, deities and the like, rather than shamans,

Of course, we can speculate to our hearts' content about the messages that were embedded in Upper Palaeolithic cave art (and some scholars feel that it is futile to even hazard a guess as to their meanings), but the truth is, we will never be able fully to read these messages, no matter how hard we try. Whether or not shamans were behind at least some of this art, what does seem certain is that the marvellous engravings and paintings found in Upper Palaeolithic caves in Europe reveal that these were places somehow perceived to be connected to a world beyond that of the living. Evidence from within the caves themselves strongly supports this theory. For example, at Lascaux in the Dordogne, which is perhaps the most celebrated of all the Upper Palaeolithic decorated caves, three ochre-covered flint blades were found thrust into a small niche in the wall located in the section of the cave known as the 'Meander'. In Enlène cave, in the Ariège region of France, hundreds of small bone pieces were found thrust into cracks in the cave wall, and it seems hard to reconcile these with any practical purpose.

At the cave of Les Trois Frères, someone entered the cave around 13,500 years ago, travelled several hundred metres along a low, narrow passage and placed the tooth of a cave bear in a niche in the wall of the small chamber featuring engravings of lions. In the same cave, in the small chamber known as the 'Chapelle de la Lionne', where there is a striking depiction of a lioness on a stalagmite flow, a bear tooth, a burnt seashell and flint tools were placed in niches in the walls. David Lewis-Williams has plausibly argued that people placed various objects in cave walls because they viewed walls as a 'membrane' between themselves and the spirit world. As he says: 'In these instances, one may possibly discern some sort of restitution ritual: two-way traffic between this world and the spirit world'. Miranda and Stephen Aldhouse-Green have noted that in several instances, Palaeolithic artists appear to have depicted animals emerging from cracks and fissures in the rock, which further points to a belief in the existence of a 'chthonic' realm beyond the cave walls.

Another interesting feature of Palaeolithic cave art, which may perhaps provide further evidence of the contact between the living and the spirit world, are the intriguing hand-prints that appear on the walls of several caves on the continent. There are two types of hand-prints: positive and negative. Positive prints were made by applying paint to the palm and fingers and then pressing the hand against cave walls, while negative prints were made by blowing paint around the outstretched hand, which was then removed to leave an image of the hand. There are also the so-called finger-flutings to consider, which are found in many continental caves. These were made when people ran their fingers (and probably also flint blades, sticks, and other implements) through mud, clay, or a substance called 'moon milk' (a precipitate of limestone) on cave walls and ceilings; making various patterns of lines and circles and sometimes, crude animals also. A recent study of the finger-flutings found in the famous cave complex at Rouffignac in the Dordogne has revealed that children between three and seven made some of these marks. Such marks could simply reveal the presence of children at play, but whilst this is quite possible, this play may also have had ritual significance as well, and perhaps they provide us with hints of prehistoric initiation rites?

Footprints belonging to children and adolescents have also been found on several cave floors and again, these could represent their participation in rituals and ceremonies which focused on them. However, in some cases, it does seem to be the case that the footprints found in caves were indeed left by children playing in them. For example, at Fontanet in the Ariège region of south-west France, a child appears to have chased a small dog or puppy into the depths of the cave some 14,000 years ago, whilst at Niaux in the same region, children probably tried to outdo each other by seeing who could make the most perfect footprints in the muddy cave floor. Paul Bahn has rightly said that such evidence shows that 'Children were clearly not afraid to explore the far depths, narrow passages and tiny chambers of caverns … whether alone or with adults'.

Leaving aside these poignant reminders of Upper

Palaeolithic life, it should be pointed out that there are numerous ethnographic accounts from around the world, which reveal how many small-scale societies often viewed (and in some cases, still view) caves as sacred places associated with supernatural powers, providing portals to the other worlds that they inhabited. The ancient Maya, for instance, viewed caves as entrances to the underworld, and the homes of powerful deities such as the rain god *Chac*. Archaeological investigations at Mayan cave sites have also revealed that people left agricultural products such as corn, chilli, and cacao seeds as ritual offerings to *Chac* and other deities. It is evident that it was not just food that was offered to the gods, as many Mayan caves also contain skeletal remains, and sadly, these show that children were often sacrificed. In far western North America (i.e. Southern California and the Great Basin), archaeology and ethnography have provided plentiful evidence of the sacred role caves played amongst the native Indian cultures of this region. Again, they were seen as entrances to the supernatural world and places where supernatural beings resided. Shamans also often went on 'vision quests' to these caves in order to make contact with their animal 'spirit helpers', who would help them enter the supernatural realm. It is also known that many of the rock paintings that can still be seen at numerous caves in far western North America were painted by shamans who visited caves on these vision quests. In northern Finland, the native Lapps (Saami) sacrificed animals and made various offerings at caves and other distinctive places in the landscape, which were seen as locations where it was possible to make contact with the supernatural world.

We will never know the exact reasoning that may have led an individual to enter Cat Hole Cave on the Gower all those thousands of years ago, and make a small and rather crude engraving of a reindeer in a dark and hidden corner of the cave. However, at the very least, if this engraving is indeed authentic then it surely tells us that the cave – like many other decorated examples in Upper Palaeolithic Europe – was perceived as a sacred place associated with the deities and spirits of this distant time. It is also quite possible that the Upper Palaeolithic people who entered Cat Hole also believed that these supernatural beings lived in another world that lay behind its cold and silent walls.

The Kendrick's Cave Mandible

Like cave art, Upper Palaeolithic portable art is also rare in Britain, but again, Wales has probably provided us with a rare and significant example of mobiliary art in the form of the Kendrick's Cave horse mandible or jawbone. I say 'probably' because this object has been dated to c.10,000 BC, which marks the very transition between the Late Upper Palaeolithic and Early Mesolithic. However, the decorated animal teeth that were also found in the cave have provided a radiocarbon date of c.11,000–10,500 BC, and as these may well have been deposited in the cave with the mandible, then a Late Upper Palaeolithic date for the latter is perhaps more likely.

The cave is located on the southern side of the Great Orme headland at Llandudno, and actually consists of an upper and lower level, with the former level being the most archaeologically productive. The cave takes its name from Thomas Kendrick, who lived in the cave after he retired from copper mining, and who discovered its prehistoric significance by accident when he enlarged his troglodytic dwelling in 1880 to make it more commodious. Kendrick also found human bones (probably the remains of three adults and a child), and although it is not certain, due to the unscientific nature of Kendrick's 'excavation', the decorated mandible may have been buried with one or more of these people. Perhaps also accompanying the dead into the next world were the oyster shell, and worked small boulders or 'hand hammers' that were recorded as having been found with the mandible. It is quite possible, that as at Goat's Hole, Paviland, Upper Palaeolithic people used Kendrick's Cave to bury their dead because it was deemed to be a 'holy' place, and, in fact, there is very little evidence to suggest that the cave was actually lived in.

The mandible is decorated with four blocks of carefully incised zigzag or herringbone pattern and a single block of ten chevrons placed one above the other, which were probably made using more than one flint tool, as the zigzag engravings are square in cross-section, while the cross-section of the chevrons is V-shaped (a sharp flint knife may have been used to cut these). The exact meaning of the

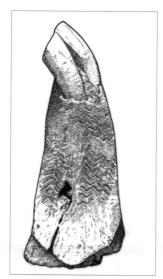

Decorated horse mandible from Kendrick's (Upper) Cave (Author)

decoration is, of course, lost to us, and it may well have had none whatsoever. However, it seems more likely that it had some ritualistic or 'magical' significance, given the fact that the mandible was deliberately deposited in Kendrick's Cave, and that it quite probably also accompanied a Late Upper Palaeolithic burial. The zigzag motif appears frequently in both portable and cave art in the Upper Palaeolithic, and David Lewis-Williams and Thomas Dowson have argued that it forms part of a suite of common motifs, which represent 'entopic phenomena' which were 'seen' by people who had somehow entered altered states of consciousness.

Also perhaps accompanying the mandible in the same burial were the decorated animal teeth mentioned above, and as far as I am aware, no other Late Upper Palaeolithic examples are known from Britain. There are nine teeth in total, and they are likely to have belonged to wild cattle and red deer. Eight of the nine teeth are decorated with transverse lines, and all are perforated with small holes, revealing that they were once worn by someone, probably as a necklace. Some of the teeth had faint traces of red ochre still on them, and it will be recalled that red ochre was used in the burial of the Red Lady of Paviland at Goat's Hole Cave. A pierced and decorated wolf canine was also found during more recent investigation of the cave in 1978, and

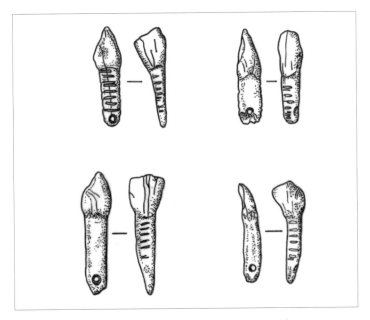

Decorated cattle and red deer teeth from Kendrick's Cave
(Redrawn after Lynch et al)

two pierced and decorated bear teeth (now unfortunately lost) were recorded by Boyd Dawkins in the nineteenth century.

Traces of red ochre were found on the intriguing animal bones (perhaps from deer) also recovered from Kendrick's Cave, which were decorated with what look like tally marks. Whether they actually were tally marks is obviously impossible to prove, but Brian Hayden and Suzanne Villeneuve have made the interesting suggestion that similar marks seen on other Upper Palaeolithic portable objects might have been used to keep records of feasting events. As they say:

> Feasting can place pressures on individuals and groups to develop some form of record-keeping system in order to keep track of the large quantities of food or gifts that are often given away at these events creating reciprocal debts that had to be paid back.

This idea may be lent some weight by the fact that in many 'traditional' societies, objects such as sticks, clay pebbles, and knotted strings were often used as notational devices to keep a record of the debts owed to individuals or communities. Alternatively, it could perhaps even be possible that the marks record an astronomical event. It is suspected that at least some Upper Palaeolithic portable art objects were used in this way – for example, an engraved bone found at the Abri Blanchard cave in the Dordogne Valley, features a series of notches that may provide a complicated record of the different setting positions of the moon at the Vernal Equinox. Whatever the true meaning of the Kendrick's Cave 'tally' marks, one of the bones on which they were made has recently been dated by AMS (Accelerator Mass Spectrometry) to around 11,800 years

ago, and so we can place them firmly in the Late Upper
Palaeolithic.

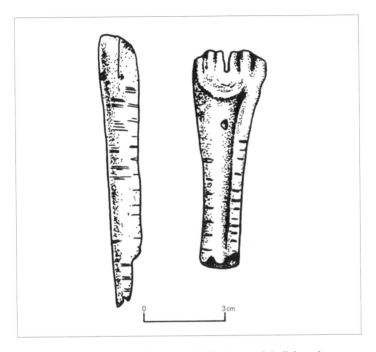

Cattle or deer bones from Kendrick's Cave with 'tally' marks
(Redrawn after Sieveking)

Prehistoric artefacts of later periods were also recovered
from Kendrick's Cave. They include a Neolithic stone axe,
an Iron Age bone comb, and a small stone axe or knife,
which may have originated in Cornwall. These artefacts
could indicate that the cave was lived in by later prehistoric
peoples, or alternatively, that it continued to be a sacred
feature of the northern Welsh landscape, long after Upper
Palaeolithic communities buried their dead here.

Chapter 4

Lost Lakes and Mesolithic Sites

Lakes would have been of considerable importance to Britain's Mesolithic communities. Not only would they obviously have provided water, but they would also have been good sources of food. Large game such as deer, which would have gathered at their edges to drink, could be hunted, along with the wildfowl populations that lakes supported, and of course, freshwater fish could also be caught from their depths. Additionally, edible aquatic plants, and reeds and rushes that could be used for domestic purposes could also have been gathered from around the edges of lakes.

The importance of lakes to Mesolithic people in Britain is nowhere more vividly illustrated than at the site of Starr Carr in the Vale of Pickering, north-east Yorkshire. This famous site was excavated by the Cambridge scholar Grahame Clark between 1949 and 1951. He uncovered a wealth of fascinating archaeological material relating to this former Mesolithic lakeside camp or 'settlement' (as we saw in the introduction, what appears to be a house has been found here), which was occupied by various Mesolithic groups during recent excavations at the site for some 500 years from between *c*.10,700–10,350 BP.

Unsurprisingly, lithic artefacts survived in the greatest abundance at the site, and amongst these were thousands of small flints or 'microliths', which Mesolithic people often fitted as barbs and points into composite spears and arrows made from wood, bone or antler. However, at Starr Carr, most of the spearheads took the form of barbed antler points, and many of the microliths and other flint tools found at the site were either used in the production of these spear-points, or were employed in other tasks such as scraping the fat off animal skins, or punching holes through prepared animal hides. It should be pointed out that the majority of the antler points at Starr Carr were unbroken and these seem to have been deliberately deposited in the edge of the former lake. Therefore, it is quite conceivable that they represent some long-lost Mesolithic ritual carried out here. Richard Chatterton has suggested that the deposition of the antler points 'may have involved actions which were designed to offer respect to animals

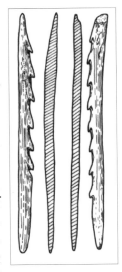

Barbed antler points from Starr Carr
(Redrawn after Clark)

killed, either through a taboo against reuse or in the regeneration and maintenance of the animal kingdom from which the slain animals came'. As he further notes, a common belief among current hunter-gatherers in North America and Eurasia is that if killed animals are offered respect, then they will be more likely to 'offer' themselves to future hunters in a reciprocal act.

Amongst the large quantities of waterlogged wood that were also found at Starr Carr, were pieces that may have belonged to a former platform built on the edge of the lake. It is quite possible that this platform may have been used for religious ceremonies at the lake edge, some of which may well have featured the votive deposition (offerings made to spirits and deities of the under/other world) of artefacts such as the antler points mentioned above.

It is apparent that the various Mesolithic communities of

Starr Carr hunted different animals, with wild cattle (aurochs), elk, red and roe deer, and wild pig featuring on the Mesolithic menu. It is perhaps not surprising that over half the animal bones come from wild cattle, as these great beasts would not have been as nimble as their more fleet-footed counterparts when it came to the hunt, although they would have been more dangerous. Remarkably, later analysis of the animal bones has found evidence of healed lesions caused by flint arrows or spears on the shoulder bones of two elk and one red deer. These lesions show that the animals in question had evaded Mesolithic hunters at least once before they met their fate. There can be little doubt that projectile weaponry played an important part in the hunting carried out during the Mesolithic, but it is also evident that the spear and bow were sometimes used to kill human rather than animal quarry. For example, at the well-known and important Late Mesolithic cemetery at Téviec in Brittany, a young adult male found in one of the graves had microlith fragments embedded in his spine, and he also had a healed fracture of the jaw. Two females who were buried in a double grave at Téviec also died violently, as evidenced by their head injuries and the arrow impact marks seen on their skeletons. Such discoveries do not prove that Mesolithic hunter-gatherers were constantly at 'war' with one another, but they do show that at least occasionally, life could be bloody and brutal during this time.

Interestingly, the remains of what appear to be domestic dogs were also discovered during Clark's investigations, and it should also be noted that part of the mandible of a small Mesolithic dog (perhaps akin to a terrier) has been recorded at Potter's Cave on Caldey Island, Pembrokeshire. Such fascinating finds reveal that 'man's best friend' has been around for many thousands of years in Britain and it is quite possible that Mesolithic people used dogs in hunting.

Undoubtedly, though, the most intriguing artefacts to be recovered during Clark's excavations were the twenty-one skull fragments or 'frontlets' from red deer, some of which still had their antlers attached. It seems highly likely that the frontlets were actually meant to be worn by people, as several of them still featured sets of two or four holes, through which securing straps of some sort were very probably passed. As to the purpose of these highly intriguing artefacts, we can only speculate, but Clark suggested in the excavation report they may well have served as headdresses in some kind of ritual dance – perhaps one which was carried out by shamans in order to increase the luck of hunters and the fertility of the deer. It is a attractive idea, and as Clark mentions, Tungu shamans in Siberia wore head-dresses made from reindeer antler, and horned deities were part of the ancient Celtic pantheon, with Cernunnos providing the most notable example.

Interestingly, in the Staffordshire village of Abbot's Bromley the men of the village still perform an annual dance in which they carry and wear crowns of reindeer antler. It seems very likely that the origins of this ritual lie deep in the prehistoric past, long before Christianity arrived to wipe out or usurp many of the old pagan traditions. However, it could be that the Starr Carr headdresses were used as disguises by hunters when stalking deer, as there are actually recorded examples from the ethnographic record of deer skins and antlers being used as camouflage by hunters (for instance, among the Apache). Of course, it is quite possible that the Starr Carr antler headdresses functioned as both shamanistic head-dresses and practical hunting devices, and as in current hunter-gatherer societies, the boundaries between the ritual and secular worlds were blurred.

Archaeological evidence for Mesolithic settlement and activity at post-glacial lakes has also been found in Wales.

These sites may be few in number (though it seems likely that there are more waiting to be found) and have produced a limited range of artefacts, but they provide us with important and fascinating insights into the Mesolithic groups who wandered the Welsh countryside several millennia ago.

Saint James' Street: Monmouth

The first site to be examined is also the most recent one discovered, and came to light during the digging of service trenches in the middle of Monmouth in December 2010, revealing that the origins of this attractive Welsh border town can be traced back a very long way. Along with other archaeological material of a later date, worked Mesolithic flints were found at three locations in the town: Saint James' Street, Wyebridge Street and Glendower Street, although the major assemblage came from the first of these locations. In the trenches, Steve Clarke and his team from Monmouth Archaeology found an end-scraper, narrow-blade microliths, waste flakes, and flint cores from which the tools had probably been struck. Dr. Elizabeth Walker, Curator of Palaeolithic and Mesolithic Archaeology at the National Museum of Wales in Cardiff, examined the finds from Saint James' Street and concluded that they were of a later Mesolithic date, dating to around 8000 BP or later. As she also says, although there are no pieces in the assemblages from the Weybridge Sreet and Glendower Street that are diagnostic of the Late Mesolithic, it is quite possible that they too, date to this time. Also found at Saint James' Street were part of a sea shell (perhaps speaking of hunting and gathering trips to the coast), an unidentifiable bone fragment; two very straight voids or hollows that may have once held wooden objects of some sort were also found in the bottom of the excavation trench.

Originally, it was felt that the Mesolithic remains found at Saint James' Street pointed to the existence of a former riverside camp located along the Wye, which would then have taken a different route through the landscape. However, Gordon McDonald (a surveyor who has undertaken detailed research on the lost lakes of the Wye valley) has suggested that although the Wye is likely to have occupied a different course in the Mesolithic, it is more likely that the camp was located on the shore of a former post-glacial lake.

Reconstruction drawing of Mesolithic camp at Monmouth
(Steve Clarke/Monmouth Archaeology)

Boncyn Ddol

In recent years, as part of a wider project funded by 'Cadw' ('cadw' = 'to keep/preserve' in Welsh), Gwynedd Archaeological Trust undertook a project to reassess all the known lithic scatters (dating from the Upper Palaeolithic to the Bronze Age) from north-western Wales. One of the project's main aims was to identify – through these scatters – possible sites of earlier prehistoric settlement, which could then be evaluated in terms of their future research potential and their need for protection.

Among the sites identified was the mound or knoll known as Boncyn Ddol, on a long and low ridge that is now under pastureland in the beautiful Upper Lledr Valley (a tributary of the Conwy), not far from the impressive remains of Dolwyddelan castle. This was one of the seats of Llywelyn the Great, prince of Gwynedd and eventually of most of Wales, who died on 11 April 1240. Boncyn Ddol, and the ridge on which it sits, was formed as a glacier moved down the valley, its massive power smoothing and sculpting the underlying landscape (Boncyn Ddol provides us with an example of what geologists refer to as a *'roche moutonne'*). Over the years, Robin and Judy Robbins have gathered a collection of Mesolithic flint tools not only from Boncyn Ddol, but also from the nearby sites of Ty'n Ddol Quarry and Ty'n Ddol, although it is Boncyn Ddol which has produced the majority of the finds. These range in date from the Early Mesolithic to the Late Mesolithic, although a few later lithics from later prehistoric periods have also been recovered from the site. Apart from a few cores and end-scrapers, most of the Mesolithic tools gathered from Boncyn Ddol and the other nearby sites take the form of flint microliths.

The lithics clearly show that Mesolithic hunter-gatherers were active at Boncyn Ddol and the other sites over several millennia, and as George Smith of Gwynedd Archaeological Trust has suggested, they may represent the ancient remnants of summer camps occupied by these groups. This idea gains further weight when we consider that the evidence for Mesolithic activity in this area is located not only close to Afon Lledr, but very probably a dried-up post-glacial lake also, both of which would have provided ready sources of food and water. In fact, as George Smith has also pointed out, the microliths found here are likely to have been used as projectiles by Mesolithic hunters. Evidence that later prehistoric hunters also visited this area may be provided by a fragment from a flint leaf-shaped arrowhead, a Late Neolithic oblique arrowhead, and a possible Early Bronze Age scraper that have also been found here. In addition to these finds, possible evidence for Bronze Age settlement (dating to around 1600 BC) was uncovered when eight small pits (1 metre square) were excavated at the eastern end of Boncyn Ddol in 1996 and 1997. Charcoal, burnt clay and stones were recovered from these pits, and possible post-holes from a structure of some sort were also found.

Pictorial evidence for the existence of the above lake comes in the form of two late sixteenth- and early seventeenth-century maps, both of which show a lake – Llyn Dolathelan – in the valley in which Boncyn Ddol is located. It seems that the lake was drained at some point in the eighteenth century, for it is not shown on a map of the area dating to 1795 or on the later first edition Ordnance Survey map published in 1840. In addition to the pictorial evidence provided by the earlier maps, there is the fact that a deep peat bed with well-defined edges lies just below Boncyn Ddol, and it thus appears likely that this peat bed marks the remnants of the former lake.

Waun Fignen Felen

As interesting as the above two sites are, it is at Waun Fignen Felen in the Brecon Beacons (*Bannau Brycheiniog*) that the clearest evidence for Mesolithic activity at a lost Welsh lake has been found. The bog is located in the wild and lonely uplands at the end of the Black Mountain (*Mynydd Ddu*) range and lies at an altitude of some 500 metres. Palae-ecological investigations at the site indicated that a shallow lake, about 300 metres long and 200 metres wide, formed around 10,000 BP with reedswamp vegetation (rushes) gradually infilling it, until finally the lake was buried beneath a layer of blanket peat which formed around 6,200 years ago. These investigations have also shown that stands of hazel woodland were present around the lake when the first Mesolithic hunters arrived here about 9,000 years ago.

Chance finds of Mesolithic lithics at Waun Fignen Felen had hinted at its possible archaeological potential, but its true significance became apparent only after Clywd-Powys Archaeological Trust carried out a survey at the site in 1979. Subsequently, the former lake became the focus of more intensive archaeological investigations, with P. Berridge directing further fieldwork at the site from 1979 to 1982,

Early Mesolithic site Waun Fignen Felen 8 under excavation
(Nick Barton)

and also in 1985, during which time several lithic scatters were studied in detail. In addition to this work, Nick Barton directed a two-week excavation at Waun Fignen Felen during May 1992 and his work has further helped to elucidate our picture of Mesolithic life in the uplands of mid Wales.

Examining the many hundreds of lithic artefacts that were found on the site, it is evident that hunter-gatherers were visiting the lake throughout the Mesolithic, as lithic scatters contained flint tools that can be firmly ascribed to both the Early and Late Mesolithic. Included amongst these tools were numerous microliths, a flint core, end-scrapers, piercing tools, and interestingly, also evidence of personal

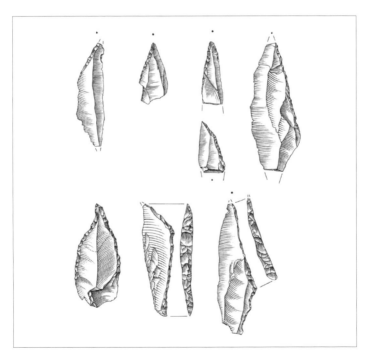

Early Mesolithic microliths from Waun Fignen Felen 8
(Nick Barton)

decoration in the form of two perforated beads (one of which was broken) made from an unusual spotted mudstone. It might be that because of the uncommon mudstone from which they were made, these beads were seen as having a magical significance by their wearer – as Stephen Aldhouse-Green has interestingly suggested. Evidence that the beads were made on site may be provided by a flint drill-bit or *mèche de forêt* that was also found, and perhaps they were even made by a Mesolithic hunter to help pass the time as he lay, bored, waiting for game to arrive at the Lake. In contrast to the Early Mesolithic lithic scatters, the later Mesolithic ones at Waun Fignen Felen contained narrow-blade microliths, which archaeologists reckon replaced broad-blade microlithic tools around 8,500 BP.

Three different types of raw materials were used to make the stone tools found at Waun Fignen Felen: Cretaceous flint, Greensand chert, and a grey-black Carboniferous chert. Interestingly, although the latter raw material occurs in the locality of the former lake, it is likely that the other two were obtained from considerable distances away. Although the Cretaceous flint may have been gathered from river gravels in the Tawe, which lies just below Waun Fignen Felen, the archaeologists who investigated the site feel that it is more probable that it was gathered from beaches on the south coast of Wales, with the nearest one located some 20 miles away. The Greensand Chert source appears to have been even further away from the site, as it is thought that it probably came from a location near Bristol, some 50 miles to the south.

However, it was the mudstone beads that travelled the furthest distance with the Mesolithic people who visited the prehistoric lake. A thin section was taken from the broken bead and this was subjected to petrographic analysis, with the results of this analysis suggesting that the nearest source of mudstone for the beads was Pembrokeshire, which is located about 62 miles from Waun Fignen Felen. As we will see in the next chapter, there is evidence to suggest that these beads may well have been made at the well-known Mesolithic site at The Nab Head, which lies on the west coast of Pembrokeshire.

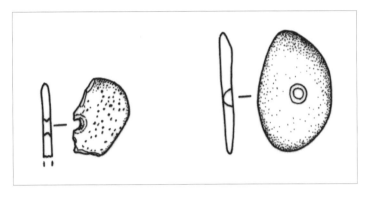

Perforated mudstone beads from Waun Fignen Felen
(Redrawn after Barton et al)

It is also interesting to note that many of the Mesolithic implements found at Waun Fignen Felen were not transported to the site ready-made, but rather, the nodules of flint and chert which provided the raw materials for them were brought to the site. If, as appears more likely, two of the three raw material sources were located at considerable distances from the lake, then, as Nick Barton and his colleagues have rightly pointed out, this suggests that Mesolithic people must have put some effort into their transportation to the lake. As they have also noted, whilst it could be argued that the nodules were moved along trade and exchange networks, the archaeological record has shown that often, flint and chert sources were often modified or reduced in some way at source to ease their transport, and there is no evidence for this to be found at Waun Fignen Felen.

Mesolithic Hunters at Waun Fignen Felen

It is probable that the lake at Waun Fignen Felen had probably become somewhat overgrown with reeds by the time Mesolithic communities first arrived in the Brecon Beacons, and also, it is likely that it was not filled with water on a permanent basis. Nevertheless, the lake would have been attractive to Mesolithic hunters as it would have provided a home for marsh birds and waterfowl, and the reeds bordering the lake edge would have provided good cover for stalking these birds and larger game. In fact, the archaeological evidence found at Waun Fignen Felen does support the idea that the lake, or lake marsh, was primarily a focus of Mesolithic hunting activity, and was occupied only briefly by the hunters who came here thousands of years ago. That this was the case is strongly indicated by the lack of any evidence for dwellings (post-holes and hearths, for example) around the lake, and by the location and nature of the various flint scatters found here. The majority of these are located at one end of Waun Fignen Felen, on its north and north-eastern edges, which, because of the prevailing wind patterns at the site, mark the windward side of the former lake. This suggests a deliberate decision on the part of hunters, as their scent, and that of any butchered animals, would have been carried away from any potential prey.

Furthermore, many of the flint and chert scatters at Waun Fignen Felen only contain small amounts of 'debitage' (waste flakes from the production of tools). This strongly indicates that the microliths and other implements were made in single or short episodes of activity, probably to be used immediately, or very soon after their production. It should also be mentioned that some of the later Mesolithic scatters appear to represent the existence of ready-made implements brought to the lake, as small groups of microliths, which are not associated with any debitage, have been found during the archaeological investigation of Waun Fignen Felen. Although it cannot be proved, it appears likely that at least some of these small tools were once slotted into actual wooden arrow or spear-shafts, which have long since rotted away. Interestingly, several microlith fragments were found in a location that was probably originally submerged near the edge of the lake. As it is felt that these were once part of a composite arrowhead, it is quite possible that they provide us with a fascinating glimpse of a Mesolithic hunter who may have shot wide with his bow

Mesolithic hunters could also have used to their advantage the narrow and deep gorge of the river Haffes, which would have allowed them to get fairly close to any prey without being seen, and to approach the lake from an upwind direction. One such hunter may actually have stopped to make or modify a weapon here, as a piece of Greensand chert debitage was found near the top of the gorge. This find may be slight, but nevertheless, it still brings us into fascinating contact with an individual from one of the Mesolithic communities who once wandered amongst the prehistoric landscapes of the Brecon Beacons.

Chapter 5

Hunter-Gatherers in Pembrokeshire

The beautiful county of Pembrokeshire (*Sir Benfro*) in south-western Wales has a rich archaeological heritage that includes several important hunter-gatherer sites such as Ogof-yr-Ychen (*ogof*: cave; *ychen*: oxen) on Caldey Island (*Ynys Byr*). It should be pointed out that Caldey Island would actually have been a hill that lay inland during the Upper Palaeolithic and Mesolithic. In fact, during the Upper Palaeolithic, Caldey 'Island' probably lay around 60 kilometres from the coast, though by the Mesolithic, it is likely to have been located only about 3 kilometres away. Ogof-yr-Ychen appears to have been used as a Mesolithic 'cemetery', because the remains of several people (at least six) have been found here. AMS dates obtained from the bones reveal that they were deposited in the cave in around 8,600–7,800 BP (although not all of the bones may represent formal burial in the cave, with some perhaps falling, or washed into the cave). Further scientific analysis carried out on the bones showed that however these Mesolithic individuals had come to find their final resting place in the cave, they had had a diet rich in seafood (with seals perhaps providing much of their protein) and must have belonged to a coastal community.

Rick Schulting and Michael Richards have pointed out that although the seafood-rich diet of the Ogof-yr-Ychen people does not prove that they lived in a permanent settlement on the coast, it does strongly suggest that not all Mesolithic communities in Wales felt the need to move away from the coast to undertake seasonal hunting and gathering trips inland. Also found in the cave were a few possible Late Upper Palaeolithic stone tools, and the bones belonging to several species of animals, some of which had long since disappeared from the landscape by the time Mesolithic hunter-gatherers arrived in the area. Included amongst the animal bones were those belonging to woolly rhinoceros, hyena, brown bear, wild cat, wolf, reindeer, bison, and aurochs. A radiocarbon date was obtained from one of the rhinoceros bones and produced a date between 23,000 and 22,000 BP.

Nana's Cave

Ogof-yr-Ychen does not stand alone, however, as there several other sites on Caldey that have produced further fascinating evidence for the prehistoric hunter-gatherers who once lived here, and there can be little doubt that Nana's Cave counts among the most important of these sites. The cave lies only about 100 metres to the north-west of Ogof-yr-Ychen and was partially excavated in 1911 by J. Coates Carter and W. Clark. Unfortunately, the two men were not exactly assiduous in their recording of the different layers of archaeology found in the cave; thus it is hard to gain a clear picture of past human activity here. As Andrew David has said in regard to Carter and Clark's work at the cave: 'Prior to its first rifling in 1911, this cave must have contained a highly informative stratigraphy covering much of the time since the last ice age'.

Nonetheless, the two men did recover human skeletal material representing the remains of three adults and at least one child. The bones (a skull and limb bones) of two of the individuals were encrusted in stalagmite and A. L. Leach, who carried out further excavations at the cave in the summer of 1915, realised that these bones had originally lain between the later prehistoric layer and the earliest basal deposits. As it now believed that there is a strong possibility that this basal layer is Late Upper Palaeolithic in date (perhaps dating to about 12,000 BP), there is thus a good chance that these two individuals represent burials of an Early Mesolithic date. The fact that a few microliths were also found in this layer may lend some support to this view, although possible Upper Palaeolithic stone tools were also found. Numerous mussel shells were also unearthed during Leach's excavations; these were probably left in a midden that formed when the cave was being used by Mesolithic people.

There cannot be many archaeological sites in Britain that have been excavated by a member of a monastic community, but in the early 1950s Frère Marie-Jaques Van Nédervelde of the Cistercian community of Caldey Abbey was given the responsibility of carrying out further excavations at Nanna's Cave by A. D. Lacaille and the renowned Welsh archaeologist, W. F. Grimes. In fact, it is evident that as well as being a man of God, the lay-brother was also something of a talented archaeologist, who did much to uncover the prehistory of Caldey. Lille and Grimes have said in respect of Brother Jaques (as he was known):

The member of the community, who, with an extraordinary flair for prehistory, laboured so diligently for three and a half years, locating sites and keeping in constant touch with us, and who proved a remarkably able and discerning pupil, is Frère Marie-Jaques Van Nédervelde.

This somewhat intriguing monk-cum-archaeologist discovered many lithic artefacts during his four seasons of work at the cave and the platform outside it, including several microliths and many fine examples of Upper

Palaeolithic tools. He also recovered several bone and stone artefacts of uncertain purpose, which included small, narrow fragments of worked bone featuring concave grooves. These implements find close parallels with antler and bone objects found at sites of the Mesolithic 'Obanian culture' in Scotland. Also found were a pig's tooth and antler tip that had been sharpened to make needle-like objects, and a narrow, finger-like beach pebble featuring signs of working on its ends. Earlier archaeologists referred to these worked pebbles as 'limpet scoops' or 'limpet hammers', and they have been found at many Mesolithic coastal sites along the Atlantic seaboard of Britain, from Alderney in the Channel Islands to the west coast of Scotland (where thousands of these artefacts have been found). However, although it is possible that in some cases these objects were used as tools for scraping shellfish from their shells, or for bashing limpets from rocks, archaeologists now prefer to use the term 'bevelled pebbles', as they come in many different shapes and sizes – suggesting that they had a range of functions. Andrew David, Palaeolothic and Mesolithic scholar, has suggested that the pebbles may have been used primarily as tanning and softening tools in the preparation of seal pelts, but also noted that some examples bear a strong resemblance to the 'plain stone chisels' that were used by the Australian Aborigines as wood-working tools. In a similar vein, Roger Jacobi feels that the bevelled pebbles closely resemble the 'finger-stones' that are though to have been used by members of the Beaker culture (about 2550–2000 BC) in leatherworking.

Daylight Rock
During 1951 and 1952 Frère Jaques was also responsible for the first archaeological excavations at the Daylight Rock site, which is located about 500 hundred metres to the

north-east of Nanna's Cave on a rugged headland on Caldey. The site consists of a small cave and sheltered slope that sit at the foot of a small inland cliff. Around thirty Mesolithic lithics, small perforated sea-shells and human bones, which included skull fragments and a robust jaw still containing several teeth and the jaw of a small child, were unearthed during the excavations in 1951 and 1952. An AMS date recently obtained from one of the bones indicates that it belonged to an individual who died around 9,000 years ago.

The sloping area outside the cave, however, was much more forthcoming in regard to the tools that were used by Mesolithic people as they went about their everyday lives. Brother Jaques found some 7,500 flint and flaked stone artefacts here. Included amongst the lithic assemblage were microliths, end-scrapers, awls or drill bits (also known as 'mèches de forêt'); and in 1969 he discovered a further hundred lithics at the site. In their account of the site in *Archaeologia Cambrensis* (1955) A. D. Lacaille and W. F. Grimes also mention that:

> Evidence of contemporary occupations just outside the cave is provided by a fairly wide patch of refuse, [which included] patinated flints ... charcoal, an admixture of broken bones and the friable vestiges of marine and terrestrial molluscan shells.

Not unjustifiably, Lacaille and Grimes felt that this midden was left behind by the Mesolithic people who had lived and worked at the site and say:

> The place, however, besides being a factory, was also the occupation site of food-gatherers, as is, of course, demonstrated by the numerous burnt flints, charcoal,

and other domestic refuse found over all the excavated area.

However, the late Roger Jacobi (an authority on Palaeolithic and Mesolithic Britain) cast doubt on the date of this presumed Mesolithic midden. He argued that the presence of shells belonging to *Helix aspersa* and *Discus rotundatus* land snails suggest that at the earliest, the midden is Roman in date (presumably these species of snail were not around in the Mesolithic – the former species is the bane of many a modern gardener's life!). It may be worth pointing out, though, that Lacaille and Grimes make no mention of the discovery at Daylight Rock of any artefacts that are later in date than the Mesolithic.

In 1988, Andrew David renewed excavations at Daylight Rock, opening a new trench to the north-west of where Brother Jaques had conducted his work outside the cave. Unfortunately this trench was empty of any Mesolithic evidence, although eighty-seven lithic artefacts were recovered from the topsoil in its vicinity. The excavation team decided to dig a new trench on top of the headland, just above the cave and sloping area, which had previously produced such an abundance of lithics. They discovered a lithic assemblage that contained over 1,500 items (although much of the assemblage consisted of the waste flakes or debitage from the production of stone tools) and fortuitously, charred fragments of hazel nutshells, which were perfect for AMS dating. Three dates were obtained and gave an average date of about 9000 BP, which agrees with the date taken on the human bone mentioned earlier.

We are going to leave Caldey Island now and travel some 40 kilometres west to a coastal site that has produced some of the most important and fascinating evidence for hunter-gatherer life in the whole of Britain – The Nab Head.

The Nab Head

The Nab Head is a small and prominent headland located on the Skomer Peninsula near Saint Brides Bay, but during the Mesolithic it would actually have been a small hill some 6 kilometres from the coast, with the Mesolithic site located on the side of a small valley. The site's location would thus have offered its Mesolithic inhabitants easy access to the plentiful resources that both the land and sea had to offer. Strictly speaking, there are actually two Mesolithic sites on The Nab, with Nab Head I (or 'The Neck') representing an Early Mesolithic phase of occupation, and Nab Head II a Late Mesolithic one. Interest in the Mesolithic occupation of The Nab Head can be traced back to the nineteenth century when various antiquarians dug at the site, collecting numerous stone tools and some perforated shale beads, and from that time until the present thousands of lithic artefacts have also been collected as stray finds on the headland.

The Discoveries of Reverend Williams

Following on the heels of the antiquarians was the Reverend J. P. Gordon-Williams, who carried out excavations at 'The Neck' in 1925. Although he did not leave a detailed account of his work, we do know that Gordon-Williams discovered an Early Mesolithic lithic assemblage consisting of many flint tools and numerous pieces of debitage (in total, there were around 3000 lithic artefacts). He also found at least eight 'limpet scoops' and some thirty perforated beads made from a blue-grey shale. However, his most notable discovery was the carved shale object that is either a representation of a very obvious part of the male anatomy, or perhaps less likely, a female figurine. As Andrew David has mentioned, W. F. Grimes suggested that it is possible that Gordon-Williams actually forged this probable 'phallus', and as he further notes, if it is indeed a forgery, then the fierce rivalry

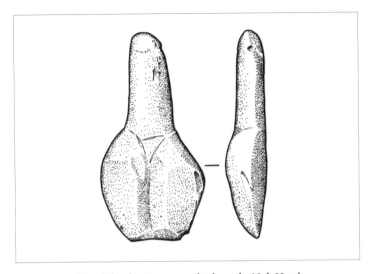

Mesolithic figurine or amulet from the Nab Head
(Redrawn after David)

that existed between local amateur collectors of prehistoric
paraphernalia may have prompted Gordon-Williams' deceit.
However, this is perhaps improbable, given that he sent the
'phallus' to be examined by another man of the church who
had a keen interest in prehistory – the famous Abbé Henri
Breuil, who, as mentioned in Chapter 2, was an eminent
scholar of Upper Palaeolithic art. The Abbé does seem to
have believed in the prehistoric authenticity of the object
(in this respect it is also worth mentioning that the object
has a very smooth surface, suggesting repeating handling),
but suggested that it was symbolic of both male and female
sexuality. He wrote back to Gordon-Williams, saying:

[It] Interests me greatly ... I checked my own
impressions by consulting others. Some call it a phallus
with exaggerated testes, others a degenerate steatopygic
figurine ... Probably both ideas are right, mixed up in a

sort of plastic play on words. The stem must be a human member with a very slight incision differentiating the glans; but the way in which the double spread out scrotum is treated is evidence of the will to bring to mind the hips and thighs and the lower belly of a woman.

Maybe the Abbé was right in his interpretation, but it could be that The Nab Head 'phallus' represents something more akin to the well-known 'Venus figurines' that have been found at several Upper Palaeolithic sites in Europe. These small sculptures, which are often very stylised, depict the naked female form, and sometimes the figures are obese, with exaggerated buttocks and breasts. The exact meaning of these intriguing statuettes is lost to us, but it could be possible that they indicate the existence of a 'mother goddess' cult, or maybe they were simply a celebration of female fertility. Andrew David has also pointed out that the profile of The Nab Head object bears some similarities to stylised engravings seen at some Upper Palaeolithic sites on the continent. It may also be worth noting that the collection of little ivory carvings that came from the site of Dolni Vestonice in southern Moravia are similar to The Nab Head piece. These diminutive objects have been viewed by many scholars as abstract female figurines, with elongated necks and exaggerated buttocks or breasts. Although such evidence comes from the Upper Palaeolithic, it perhaps suggests that we cannot rule out the possibility that there is some feminine symbolism behind the small but fascinating piece of carved shale from The Nab Head. It may be, though, that Andrew David is right when he says: 'it is perhaps more realistic to view The Nab Head object as simply a phallus, perhaps an amulet, without convenient parallel'. Of course, all such speculations on The Nab Head object may be idle, if the good Reverend did indeed forge the piece, though we will never know whether he has pulled the wool over all our eyes!

During his excavations at The Nab Head, Gordon-Williams also found a small, ovoid shale pebble which has a groove which may have been deliberately incised into in its broader end. Roger Jacobi has said that 'It would be attractive to interpret this object as a second more "elementary" Venus representation, with the vulva indicated by the incision', although it has to be said that it is not certain that this 'figurine' has even been shaped by human hands.

Twentieth-century excavations at The Nab Head

After a short trial excavation at 'The Neck' in 1979, Andrew David and D. Benson directed a more thorough investigation of the site with the Dyfed Archaeological Trust in 1980. As a result of this work, they also discovered Nab Head Site II, which was subsequently excavated during three short seasons in 1981, 1982 and 1986. A considerable quantity of new evidence was recovered during these excavations and this has undoubtedly helped to shed further fascinating light on the Mesolithic in Wales.

At 'The Neck'/The Nab Head Site I, hundreds of Early Mesolithic flint and stone tools (with pebble flint the major raw material – presumably taken from nearby beaches) were recovered from a lithic assemblage containing some 40,000 artefacts, with end-scrapers, 'broad blade' microliths and *mèches de forêts* the most dominant tool types. Also found was a transversely sharpened axe or adze, which resembles the other few examples that were found by Gordon-Williams. Sixty-four beads were also found, some of which were perforated, while others were only partially perforated or were 'blanks' that had not been drilled through. All the beads, with the exception of one example made from Old Red Sandstone, were manufactured from blue-grey shale.

Although somewhat disappointingly, no firm evidence for further carved items was found, a small cobble bearing an intriguing arrow-like motif did come to light. Although this carved stone was found in the topsoil and was not associated with any Mesolithic artefacts, it is nonetheless possible that it represents another item of Mesolithic 'artwork'.

Excavations at The Nab Head Site II also produced an abundant lithic assemblage with around 32,000 stone and flint artefacts, and again, beach pebble flint was the dominant raw material used to make tools. We cannot say for sure how this flint was gathered from nearby beaches but presumably people used bags and baskets made from organic materials which have left no trace. The most numerous tool-types were microliths and 'denticulates' (which also cropped up in small numbers at Site I), although archaeologists are a little in the dark when it comes to the function of the latter, suggesting that they may have been used as scrapers, or alternatively, as cores for microliths (or both). Fifty-five bevelled pebbles were also unearthed in many parts of the site (as well as fragments from many broken examples); and it may be interesting to note – in light of the above suggestion that they may have been used as tanning or softening tools – that the end of one example had been polished smooth through use. The most notable stone objects to be recovered from The Nab Head Site II have to be the three ground, and pecked stone axes, and the perforated stone disc; a pecked sandstone axe and two stone discs were also probably found at 'The Neck' by Lord Kensington and his brother in the late nineteenth century. These two types of artefact are not commonly found on British Mesolithic sites, and so they are important. It seems safe to assume that the axes were everyday, practical tools, and although we can only guess as to what Mesolithic people used them for, it may be that they were

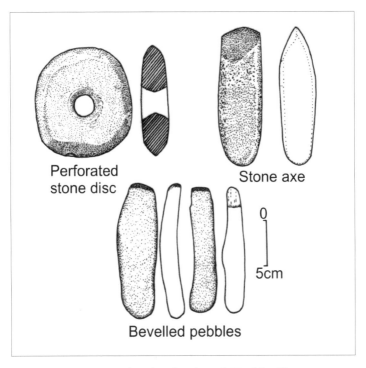

Stone artefacts found at the Nab Head Site II
(Redrawn after David)

used to scrape the subcutaneous fat of animal hides, or to dismember animal carcasses. However, it is perhaps more probable that they were mainly used as woodworking tools, although it is quite possible – and quite likely – that Mesolithic people put them to more than one use as they went about their business. The perforated stone discs are rather more enigmatic, although it could be possible that the example found at The Nab Head Site II was a macehead used as a weapon, or as a status symbol (or both).

Although no firm evidence for Mesolithic dwellings was found during the excavation of 'The Neck', hints that such structures had existed at The Nab Head Site II did come to light there. Perhaps the most telling hint was that the flint and stone tools were recovered from three distinct areas of debitage (which also included burnt flints and charcoal), which clustered around an area (about 5 metres in diameter) largely devoid of artefacts. Whether a Mesolithic dwelling had once stood in this 'empty' area may be impossible to prove, but as Stephen Aldhouse-Green has remarked that 'It is tempting to interpret the Nab Head plan as indicative of a house-site surrounded by discard zones of artefacts, burnt flint and charcoal'.

Also discovered during the excavation of The Nab Head Site II was a small pit (which had been capped by a layer of tightly fitting stones) containing burnt soil and a scattering of charcoal. It is quite possible that this feature represented the remains of a hearth (or hearth sweepings) and a piece of charcoal from the pit produced an AMS radiocarbon date of around 7300 BP. A concentration of burnt soil and charcoal lay some 6 metres to the north-west of the 'hearth', amongst a scatter of flints, many of which were burnt. It does seem likely, therefore, that this feature was also a hearth, although a dated charcoal sample from it indicated that it had been in use at towards the end of the Mesolithic about 6300 years ago. A further dated charcoal sample recovered from about 4.5 metres to the west of this probable hearth returned a date of about 8000 BP, although it is possible that this piece of charcoal could have been introduced into the site from another one elsewhere on The Nab Head. What the dated charcoal samples do strongly suggest, however, is that the The Nab Head was a focus of settlement throughout the Mesolithic.

A Mesolithic bead 'factory'
Around seven hundred Early Mesolithic beads have been found at the Nab Head, with the majority occurring as

chance finds. In addition to the beads, we also have the many drill-bits, bead 'blanks', and partially drilled beads that have been recovered from the headland. As Andrew David points out, it also seems likely that a great number of beads have been lost as a result of the erosion that has taken place at The Nab Head, and through the carelessness of earlier excavators. Although Mesolithic beads have been found at other Early Mesolithic sites in Wales (e.g. at Waun Fignen Felen) and elsewhere in Britain, they cannot compete with The Nab Head in terms of the numbers found. Thus all in all, the evidence strongly suggests that the site was a production centre or 'factory', with beads produced for personal ornamentation, either sewn into clothing or used to make bracelets necklaces, headdresses, and perhaps also to decorate personal items, such as tools and weapons. It may be that, as has been suggested for the drilled shell beads made by Native American tribes in the Mississippi River Valley, the beads from The Nab Head were worn only by high-ranking members of Mesolithic society as 'badges' of status, or were used as ritual exchange items which

Bracelet made by George Nash using original beads from the Nab Head
(George Nash)

cemented and fostered relationships with other groups. We should perhaps also bear in mind Roger Jacobi's interesting suggestion that The Nab Head beads (and the stone rings and pecked stone axes) might originally have been deposited with burials which have long since disappeared from the headland.

The Trefael Stone
(George Nash)

Intriguing evidence has been found at a later prehistoric monument in Pembrokeshire, which perhaps indicates that some Nab Head beads at least may indeed have been traded or exchanged with other Mesolithic groups in Pembrokeshire. This monument is the 'Trefael Stone', which is located not far from The Nab Head near the village of Nevern, and was excavated under the direction of George Nash in November 2010. The excavation revealed that although this hefty boulder, which was covered with some seventy-five cup-marks on its surface, had been erected in the Bronze Age as a standing stone, it had probably originally been the capstone of a small Portal Dolmen (a type of Early Neolithic tomb common along the western seaboard of Britain). Some astronomers have also suggested that the cup-marks may actually be a 'star-map', showing a part of the night sky that includes the constellations of Cassiopeia, Orion, Sirius, and the North Star.

During the excavation, two perforated beads were also recovered from a disturbed context at the site and it was felt that they are identical to examples recovered from The Nab Head. Thus it is quite possible that the perforated beads found at the Trefael Stone mark the earlier presence of Mesolithic people at the site who were in contact with their contemporaries at the Nab Head bead 'factory'. On the other hand, however, it might be the case that rather than travelling along a Mesolithic trade or exchange network, these beads actually moved with one or more Mesolithic groups (or individuals) who had once lived and worked at the Nab Head, but who had then moved from the site to these locations. I should perhaps also mention that a shale bead found on New Quay beach also closely resembled those from The Nab Head, as did the examples found at Waun Fignen Felen.

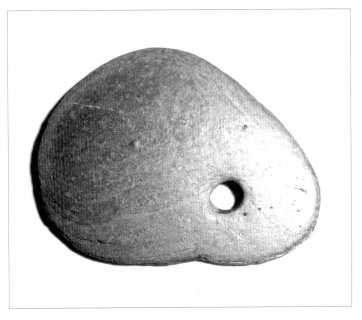

Perforated shale bead from Newquay
(George Nash)

Priory Farm Cave

Located high above the Pembroke river, this cave was first archaeologically investigated in 1906–1907 by Dr A. Hurell Style and Mr E. E. L. Dixon, who found eighteen flint and chert artefacts in the entrance area of the cave. Included amongst this small collection of lithics are four 'penknife points', which were probably hafted as spear-points or knives, a burin that may have been used to work wood and

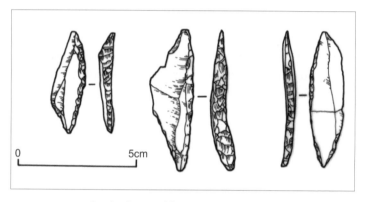

'Penknife points' from Priory Farm Cave
(Redrawn after Green and Walker)

antler, and three fragments from probable Mesolithic 'backed blades'. The presence of the penknife points indicates that a Late Upper Palaeolithic community had occupied the cave in around 12,000 BP. Bones from various species of animals (e.g. hyena, wolf, reindeer, and bear) were recovered from deeper within the cave, while an adult human skull and part of a child's jawbone were found near its entrance. Further human bones (from at least two individuals) were found inside the cave, and although the date of the human skeletal material found at the cave is unclear it does indicate use of the cave as a prehistoric burial place. Nick Barton and Catherine Price conducted new archaeological work at the cave in 1999, finding further evidence of Final Upper Palaeolithic occupation in the form of numerous small pieces of debris from flint-working.

Hoyles' Mouth and Little Hoyle Cave

These two caves are located above the Ritec Valley near Tenby and lie within 350 metres of each other. Hoyle's Mouth is the more interesting and more productive of the two caves. The first recorded excavation at the cave is that undertaken by Colonel Jervis in 1840, although a graffito reading '1817' in the deepest reaches of the cave indicates the presence of earlier explorers or fossil hunters. The cave was subsequently the subject of several more archaeological investigations in the nineteenth and twentieth centuries, and these produced quite a substantial collection of stone tools (about ninety were found, along with some 270 waste pieces) dating to the Late Upper Palaeolithic, around 12,500 BP. A 'busked burin' from the Early Upper Palaeolithic is also known to have been found at the cave, suggesting that an earlier phase of occupation took place at the cave around 30,000 BP.

It is also interesting to note that lithic artefacts have been recovered from the deepest and darkest reaches of cave, in the 'Reindeer Chamber', which lies some 40 metres from the cave entrance. Stephen Aldhouse-Green and Elizabeth have made the plausible suggestion that these finds could be associated with activity of a ritual nature, although, as they further remark, they could have been dropped by people who had been in some sort of danger and who had thus sought the security of the cave's farthest depths. It has to be said, however, that the former scenario seems the more likely of the two.

Although not as productive as its neighbour in terms of

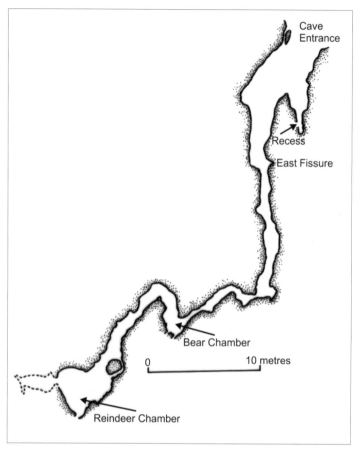

Plan of Hoyle's Mouth Cave
(Redrawn after Green and Walker)

finds, a few flint tools have been recovered from the various excavations undertaken at Little Hoyle Cave, along with a perforated bone awl or needle that was perhaps used to fashion the clothes worn by the makers of these tools. One of the flint tools – a Late Upper Palaeolithic 'convex-backed blade' – was found in association with pieces of charcoal, suggesting the former presence of a hearth within the cave.

The cave also seems to have been used as a burial place by later ancient communities in the area, as the remains of around ten people were found scattered in the filling of the central 'chimney' (a natural shaft connecting the cave to the surface above) and these were associated with Roman and later finds.

Chapter 6

Footprints from the Past

This is what we do archaeology for. I can stand exactly where a Mesolithic hunter stood, and beside me my eight-year old daughter can stand in footprints where a similar-aged child 6,000 years ago squashed her feet into the soft muds and silts of a shallow pond. Although separated by six millennia the shared human experience is almost tangible. I'm on a windswept beach in west Wales teaching my daughter about archaeology. Six thousand years ago in exactly the same place a father trained his child in hunting as they stood amongst the reeds and waited for animals to come down to drink.

Ken Murphy, Dyfed Archaeological Trust

Ken Murphy's evocative words were written in response to the discovery in 2010 of prehistoric footprints at Lydstep Haven beach, Pembrokeshire, which were preserved in the surface of a solidified peat deposit that had originally been the floor of a shallow lagoon in the Mesolithic. These footprints, which provide us with a remarkable and poignant snapshot of a day in the lives of an ancient community, were left by both adults and children, and date towards the very end of the Mesolithic, around 4,300-4000 BC. The prints were set deeply into the peat, suggesting that the people who made them had been standing waiting for something, and perhaps as Murphy has suggested, they were made by a hunting party who had hidden amongst the reeds of the lagoon, waiting to ambush any unsuspecting animals that came here to drink. Some support for this theory may be provided by the fact that red deer hoofprints were also found preserved in the peat nearby.

Almost as extraordinary as the Lydstep footprints was the discovery of a boar skeleton nearby. It was found on the beach in the summer of 1917 by Arthur Leach during his examination of submerged forest sites in Pembrokeshire. Immediately above the neck vertebrae of the skeleton were two broken microliths, which had very probably been the instruments of the animal's death; and above these, was a substantial piece of tree trunk (8 feet long and nearly 1 foot in diameter) pinning the skeleton to the ground. This evidence led earlier archaeologists to postulate that the boar had first been shot by hunters, but had then escaped only to be crushed by a falling tree! Richard Chatterton has rightly

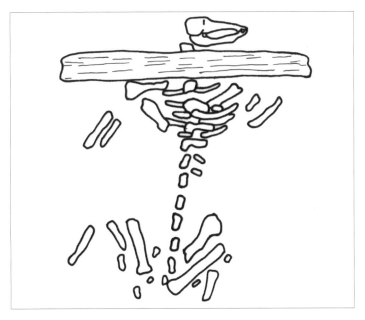

Plan of the Lydstep boar burial
(Redrawn after Coneller and Walker)

pointed out that if this did indeed happen, then the boar was 'one of the most unfortunate animals ever to have lived [and] an alternative [and more plausible] explanation could be that the animal had been killed and deliberately weighted down beneath water by the tree'. It is an attractive theory which is lent considerable support by the fact that the shells of freshwater snail shells (which were not present elsewhere at Lydstep) were found in the silt in which the skeleton was found, strongly indicating that the boar was deliberately deposited into a pool.

Chatterton has further noted that the deliberate disposal of whole animal carcasses into lakes and bogs has long been a recognised feature of the Late Upper Palaeolithic and Mesolithic on the continent, and has been identified at several sites. For example, at the well-known hunter-gatherer settlements that lie close to each other at Meiendorf (a Late Upper Palaeolithic site dating to around 10,000 BC) and Stellmoor in North Germany (an Early Mesolithic site, about 8500 BC), many reindeer carcasses were deliberately weighted down in a small lake with large stones. Aubrey Burl tells us that at the former site, people had inserted an eighteen-pound block of sparkling banded gneiss into the chest cavity of a two-year old doe reindeer, sewed up the cavity, and then deposited the carcass in the lake. It is also evident that many other of the reindeer were sent to the lake bottom carrying blocks of stone inside their thoraxes. In Scandinavia, there have also been many whole animal carcasses from the Mesolithic found in lakes and bogs, many of which must have ended up in their watery graves not by chance, but rather, by human design.

Returning to Britain, as well as the Lydstep boar, there are other probable examples of animals deliberately deposited in watery places by prehistoric hunter-gatherers. Among these is the partial skeleton (dated to 8250–7550 BC) of an aurochs (now-extinct wild cattle) and associated Late Mesolithic microliths, which seems to have been deliberately deposited in the lake edge at Seamer site B, near Starr Carr in the Vale of Pickering. At Ham Marsh, Newbury (Berkshire) an aurochs skeleton with microliths embedded in its sinus region was recovered along with a red deer horn.

There is also the Late Upper Palaeolithic elk skeleton (dated to 11,850–11,300 BC), which was found at Poulton-le-Fylde near Blackpool in a layer of alluvium that represented a former shallow lake. Although two bone barbed points found with the skeleton may have caused its death, this is not certain; it is thus possible that, like the elk, they were ritually deposited in the lake.

It was mentioned in Chapter 4 that the antler points deposited into the former lake edge at Starr Carr may have been votive deposits that were connected to hunter-gatherer beliefs about the animals they hunted. The same could therefore be true in respect of the animals that seem to have been deliberately deposited in lakes and bogs by prehistoric hunter-gatherer communities in Europe. Alternatively, it could be that rather than honouring the animals they hunted, hunter-gatherers were offering the animals to the supernatural powers that they believed lived in places such as lakes and bogs, which formed sacred points in the landscape. In fact, given that there is abundant and compelling evidence that many societies in later prehistoric Europe made votive offerings in sacred waters (with people who had been ritually murdered sometimes taking the place of objects), it would be rather surprising if earlier hunter-gatherers did not do the same. From a Welsh perspective, the assemblage of beautiful Iron Age metalwork deposited in the small lake known as Llyn Cerrig Bach, Anglesey (*Ynys Môn*), provides a particularly noteworthy example of a later prehistoric votive deposit.

It is evident that along with animals, human bones were also ritually deposited in watery places during the European Mesolithic. In southern Scandinavia, for instance, archaeologists commonly find human bones that were deposited by Mesolithic people at the edges of former lakes, while in Britain, human bones recovered from the Mesolithic sites at Thatcham (Berkshire) and Staythorpe (Nottinghamshire) probably also came from watery graves. It is also worth mentioning the remarkable discovery made at the submerged Mesolithic coastal site of Møllegabet II in Denmark. Here, Mesolithic people placed an individual in a canoe, which they then submerged just off the shoreline; intriguingly, before this boat burial was consigned to the sea, both the canoe and the body were wrapped in birch-bark.

Returning to the Lydstep 'boar', I should mention that it has been suggested – on the basis of the small size of the skeleton – it may actually be an escaped domestic pig. If this is indeed the case, it points to the existence of a very early Neolithic farming settlement somewhere in the area of Lydstep Haven, as the skeleton has since been dated to 4350–3940 BC. Although this is probably unlikely, it is certainly not impossible, particularly when it is considered that radiocarbon dates obtained from a number of Neolithic sites elsewhere in Britain indicate that the first Neolithic farming communities first appeared here during the final centuries of the fifth millennium BC. However, it should also be borne in mind that although the establishment of the Neolithic way of life in Britain probably occurred quite rapidly, it would not have been an 'instantaneous' process. In some areas of the country there must have been some overlap, with hunter-gatherers clinging on to their ancient way of life, until finally it disappeared forever, unable to compete with the relentless spread of farming.

We will never know for sure whether the Lydstep boar

(or pig) was some sort of ritual offering, and it could be that the animal escaped its hunters only to later die through loss of blood, perhaps even suffering the further misfortune of then being crushed by a falling tree trunk – though this seems highly unlikely. The true identity of the people responsible for the pig's demise will also never be known, and we can only speculate in this regard. However, as the probable boar skeleton dates to around the same time as the human footprints found nearby, could it be possible that it was killed and then ritually deposited in a small pool by the very same people who left these remarkable reminders of their prehistoric lives in the mud of the lagoon all those thousands of years ago?

Mesolithic Footprints in the Severn Estuary

Remarkably, hundreds of footprints made by Mesolithic people have also been found at three locations in the Severn Estuary, and unlike those found at Lydstep Haven they take the form of tracks or trails made by individuals as they moved across the prehistoric landscape. The first to be looked at are those found at Uskmouth and Magor Pill, near Newport (*Casnewydd*) in south-east Wales.

The footprint trails were found and investigated some twenty years ago and were situated on the present inter-tidal foreshore in estuarine clay, which was overlain by later peat deposits. The peat at Uskmouth was dated to 5460-4960 BC, providing what archaeologists call a *terminus ante quem* for the footprint tracks found here. In other words, the people who had made these prints must have done so before the peat was laid down. Likewise, at Magor Pill the footprints underlay a layer of peat, and this was dated to around 6000 BP.

The Uskmouth and Magor Pill Footprints

Three certain footprint-trails were identified at Uskmouth and they were left by three Mesolithic individuals as they walked – probably barefoot – across the foreshore of the estuary, which at the time would probably have been fringed by stands of reed swamp bordering a salt-marsh environment. Trail or Line 1 appears to have been made by a man who was probably of average stature and who would have fitted into a British shoe size 9, while examination of the footprints of Line 2 indicated that the individual – male or female – would have taken a size 8 shoe. Whether the two individuals were walking together when they made the trails is impossible to say for sure, but as the two trails were only some 10 metres apart it is quite possible that they were.

The Line III footprints were located close (about 3 metres away) to those of Line 1 but were moving in the opposite direction, toward the mouth of the Usk estuary, and they were also probably (but not definitely) made by a young boy or girl. The fact that these footprints lay near to those of Line 1 strongly suggests that these two individuals at least were together, and it is even possible that they belonged to a mischievous Mesolithic child who was running away from a parent or sibling.

About 370 metres to east of the footprint trails at Uskmouth, a perforated antler mattock was found lying on the surface of the estuarine clay of the estuary. The mattock is made from part of a reindeer antler, and it has since been radiocarbon dated to between 5268 and 4927 BC. It is thus conceivable that the mattock is contemporary with the Uskmouth footprints and maybe was even lost by the people who made them. Archaeologists are in general agreement that Mesolithic antler mattocks were probably primarily used for digging out plant foods, although the possibility that they were sometimes employed as weapons

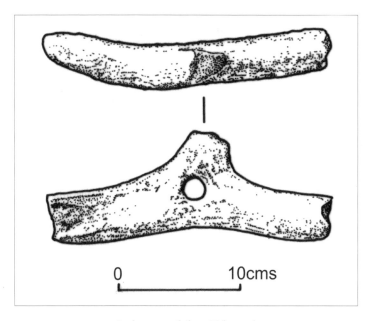

Antler mattock from Uskmouth
(Redrawn after Aldhouse-Green et al)

cannot be totally discounted. We may even have possible evidence of this with 'Cheddar Man', whose skeleton (which dates to the Early Mesolithic, *c*.8000 BC) was discovered at Gough's Cave in Cheddar Gorge, Somerset. Examination of Cheddar Man's skull revealed that he had probably received a number of vicious blows to the head from some sort of club, and one of these (between his eyes) never completely healed and probably eventually killed him. It should also be mentioned that this famous site has also yielded strong evidence pointing towards cannibalism in the Late Upper Palaeolithic

At Magor Pill, which is situated about 10 kilometres to the north-east of Uskmouth, a single footprint-trail and single footprints from former trails came to light in 1990. Again, the people who left these footprints seem to have

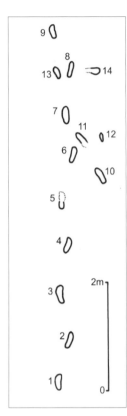

Plan of Mesolithic foot-print trail, Magor Pill (Redrawn after Aldhouse-Green et al)

been walking barefoot when they made them, and one of the prints appears to have been left by a child. The footprints in the main trail correspond to a modern shoe size 12, revealing the presence of a man who probably measured about 6 feet tall, which would have been rather unusual in the Mesolithic – or who just had very big feet!

Goldcliff East

Although Starr Carr remains the most famous and productive Mesolithic site in Britain, the site of Goldcliff East has also produced numerous strands of archaeological evidence which have thrown considerable light on the somewhat dark and mysterious world of Mesolithic Britain. Goldcliff East lies about 4 kilometres to the east of Uskmouth and actually consists of a complex of several different Mesolithic sites (Sites A–J) dating to around 6300–4800 BC, which were uncovered by Professor Martin Bell and his team during three hard but rewarding years of excavation in the muddy estuary. The sites are located on a former 'bedrock island' that would have been a striking feature in the estuary, rising at least 20 metres above the surrounding landscape. During the period of Mesolithic activity on the island, there would have been a wetland environment of saltmarsh and reed-swamp, with hazel, oak, and alder woodland also present on its fringes.

Undoubtedly, the most notable of the many fascinating discoveries made at Goldcliff East was the exceptional collection of human footprint-tracks, which had something of an impact on Neil Oliver when he visited the site. He was moved to say:

> They are almost too much, the human footprints: looking at them, touching them, felt like eavesdropping, or secretly watching someone in an unguarded moment. I had to stare at them but part of me wanted to look away, out of respect for privacy ... Our ancient past is powerful magic, strong drink – even a little shot of it can snatch your breath away and make you wonder if you can, any more, believe what you are seeing.
>
> Neil Oliver, *A History of Ancient Britain*

Hundreds of footprints (some of which may have been made as early as 6300 BC) were revealed during the excavations at Goldcliff, and some 270 of these appear to have been made by twenty-one different individuals, many of whom were children and adolescents, with the youngest children as young as three to four years old.

Close scrutiny of the footprints by Martin Bell and his team has helped to bring us even closer to the people who left these ghostly imprints of their lives in the Severn estuary. (The majority of the prints seem to have been made in the spring/summer months.) For example, four footprint-trails discovered at Site E were probably left by four individuals aged around thirteen to eighteen years old, and it seems to be the case that they were all walking together in the same direction at the same time. Furthermore, it is evident that they all paused at the same point for reason. Martin Bell has plausibly suggested that these footprints belong to a hunting party (maybe, but not definitely, consisting of young males) and that they paused to observe the animal(s) they were stalking. The most poignant footprints, however, have to be those left at Site C, where the probable footprints of a young boy or girl aged about four, randomly criss-crossed footprint-tracks made by an older boy or girl of around eleven, whose deeper tracks suggested that he or she may have been carrying a load of some sort. The lack of direction in the child's footprints suggest that he or she may have been playing or 'mud-larking', and likewise, the somewhat random pattern of the

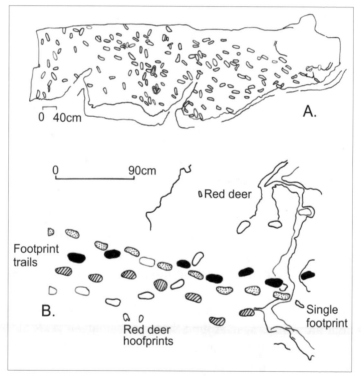

Mesolithic footprint trails from Goldcliff East
(Redrawn after Scales)

older individual's footprint-tracks suggest that he/she was also joining in the fun. Perhaps then, these two sets of footprints take us back to a day thousands of years ago when two siblings played together on the mudflats of the Severn Estuary, and maybe it is even possible that the load carried by the older child was a younger brother or sister.

Many animal tracks were also discovered during the Goldcliff excavations, with the majority left by red deer. It is interesting to note – in light of the idea that the footprints at Site E were left by a hunting party – that they were near to red deer hoof-prints. Also of some interest are the two tracks found to the west of Site C, which were probably made by a wolf that may have been running when it left them in the mud. It is perhaps possible that these tracks were left by a domesticated dog, but the former is more likely, as the tracks are very similar in size to those of a modern wolf. A wide range of bird tracks was also recorded at Goldcliff, and there was an abundance of crane and grey heron tracks, although others made by oyster catchers, black headed gulls, common gulls, and terns were also indentified.

In addition to numerous lithic artefacts found at Goldcliff, around forty pieces of worked wood (which is rarely found on British Mesolithic sites), and a smaller collection of bone and antler tools was recovered. Site J (dated 4900–4710 BC) produced the majority of the wooden artefacts, and amongst these there was a long, narrow, slightly curved piece of worked wood of uncertain purpose. It has been suggested by Martin Bell that this object may perhaps have been used as either a digging stick or as a spear, although, as he points out, the former possibility seems the more likely given its shape. Another piece of carefully-worked wood whose function was hard to pin down was a Y-shaped object, with one of its prongs apparently broken. However, as Martin Bell has pointed out, if the shaft of this artefact was originally longer, it would have provided Mesolithic people with a very useful tool for catching eels hibernating in the mud. Several other wooden artefacts of uncertain purpose were also recovered from Site J.

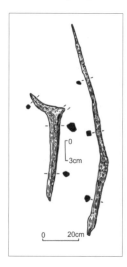

Wooden artefacts from
Goldcliff East
(Redrawn after Foster)

The bone tools discovered at Goldcliff are important, as these are generally very rare on British Mesolithic sites, with the majority coming from Starr Carr and sites of the Scottish 'Obanian' culture. They were found on Sites A, B, J, with the latter site again proving the most productive, although only around twenty bone tools were recovered from the three sites. This assemblage included an awl made on an aurochs humerus, which may well have been used to perforate skins, and several long bone shafts with 'U'-shaped ends, which were probably used for scraping animal skins. There were also a number of bones bearing butchery marks, and a particularly interesting find was the distal end of an aurochs radius (the foreleg) bearing what are either stab marks from a pointed weapon or tool, or perhaps more probably, the impact marks left by microlithic armatures that were mounted in spears or arrows.

Although it was not discovered during the excavations at Goldcliff, the late Derek Upton (who was largely responsible for realising the archaeological potential of the Severn Estuary Levels) did find an antler mattock-hammer on a gravel beach near a major concentration of footprints at Site C. The battered pedicle indicated that this T-shaped tool had been used as a hammer, and the C-shaped socket

148

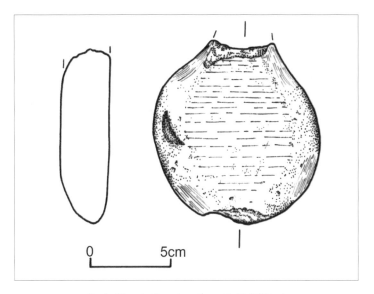

Probable grinding stone from Goldcliff East
(Redrawn after Foster)

that been hollowed out of the main beam of the antler probably originally held a stone axe/adze (two examples of these were found on the foreshore near Sites B and D) or possibly a wood point. If this artefact had indeed originally contained a stone axe/adze, as seems more likely, it would have been a useful and effective woodworking tool.

Of a more enigmatic nature than the mattock-hammer was the rounded sandstone plaque found at Site B, which may have first been used as a grinding stone to process plant foods, and also as a pounding stone. However, we cannot rule out the possibility that this object had a symbolic rather than a practical value and thus was valued by its owner as a special item.

Several heat-fractured stones were also recovered during the excavations, with the majority coming from Site J, which was probably a base camp for a small Mesolithic community. Heat-fractured stones are a common find on Mesolithic sites in Britain and elsewhere in Europe, and although it is hard to say for sure what they were used for, the ethnographic record suggests that at least in some cases these stones were used to help cook food. Interestingly, the fractures and crazing seen on many of the Goldcliff heat-fractured stones suggests that they had been used to heat water in a wooden or hide container of some sort, or perhaps in pit cooking. It is has also been suggested that Mesolithic people may also have used heat-fractured stones in prehistoric saunas and in craft activities.

As is often the way at Mesolithic sites, no clear evidence for Mesolithic dwellings was found at Goldcliff. However, three distinct concentrations of artefacts in roughly circular spreads were unearthed during the excavations, and it is possible that these define the edges of long-decayed wigwam-type structures, covered by skins or reed thatch. Some support for this idea is provided by the fact that the three spreads all measured around 3–4 metres in diameter, and furthermore, in the centre of one of these there was an area of charcoal and burnt flint flakes, suggesting the former existence of a hearth.

Chapter 7

Mesolithic Sites in North Wales

As have seen in previous chapters, evidence of Mesolithic hunter-gatherer communities has been found at Boncyn Ddol, but this is just one site among many in north Wales where evidence of Mesolithic life has been found. In this chapter we will look more closely at some of these, beginning at the popular seaside resort of Prestatyn, where a number of Mesolithic sites have come to light, with the one discovered at Nant Hall Road the most notable.

Nant Hall Road lies on the eastern side of the town, about 1 kilometre from the sea-front. The first hints of Mesolithic activity in this area were discovered in the 1920s and 1930s when F. Gilbert Smith, a local architect and keen amateur archaeologist, recovered around 500 lithics from a ploughed field just to the east of the site. Although the majority of these are Neolithic in date, several microliths were also recovered, providing firm evidence of a Mesolithic presence along this stretch of the north-Welsh coast. F. G. Smith discovered further Mesolithic material in the late 1920s during the building of the Bryn Newydd housing estate, which is located about 400 metres south of Nant Hall Road. This material included around 100 stone tools made of local chert, a perforated oyster shell disc (presumably an

Oyster shell pendant and bone point from Bryn Newydd, Prestatyn
(Redrawn after Clark)

item that once adorned someone or something), a pointed bone object, and a piece of unworked deer antler.

Similar bone artefacts were found in many of the graves at the previously mentioned famous Late Mesolithic cemeteries of Téveic and Höedic on the coast of Brittany, which have yielded much fascinating evidence for hunter-gatherer life in north-west Europe. In many cases, these artefacts were located on the chest area of the skeletons found in the graves, and so it seems likely that they were used as pins that fastened garments of some sort.

Fragments of hazelnut shells were also found at Bryn Newydd, and subsequent dating of these has revealed that they were dropped by Mesolithic people around 10,000 years ago. Around 200 Mesolithic lithics were also recovered as a result of various nineteenth- and twentieth-century excavations undertaken at a later prehistoric site and Romano-British bathhouse at Melyd Avenue, some 1.5 kilometres south-west of the centre of Prestatyn.

Returning to the Nant Hall Road site, in advance of housing development here, archaeological investigations were carried out between 1991 and 1993 by staff from Clwyd-Powys Archaeological Trust, Clwyd County Council, and the University of Wales, Lampeter. What they found provided fascinating evidence of how Late Mesolithic and Early Neolithic groups had made use of the natural resources that the nearby coastline had to offer. Six shell middens were uncovered by the archaeologists, and these date from 4200–3400 BC, with the four Late Mesolithic shell middens being primarily composed of mussel shells, and the two Neolithic ones, cockle shells. Several Late Mesolithic/Early Neolithic lithics and a small assemblage of animal bones were also recovered during the excavations, with red deer, arouchs/elk, sheep/goat, cow and wild or domestic pig identified among the latter.

The fact that the mussel middens are earlier than the cockle middens points to a changing coastal ecology in this area, as mussels generally live on rocks, while cockles live in sandy and muddy sediments. Although it is perhaps possible that the Neolithic people chose not to eat cockles for some reason, this seems unlikely, and other environmental evidence from the wider region supports the hypothesis that the ecology of the nearby coastline had changed by their time.

Perhaps the most important aspect of the Prestatyn shell middens is that they imply that along this part of the coast at least, the transition to the Neolithic was a gradual, rather drawn-out affair, with Early Neolithic communities essentially following a similar lifestyle to their Mesolithic predecessors. However, although hunting and gathering may well have been of greater importance to these people, the presence of wheat and barley grains found in association with the cockle middens suggests that they were also cultivating cereal crops, probably in small clearings created within the woodland that fringed the coast.

I should perhaps also mention the skeleton of a young woman, which was discovered in 1942 by workmen digging on Prestatyn High Street. Recent dating of the skeleton suggests that the young woman died around 3600 BC, although it is hard to say for sure if she was intentionally buried, as there was no sign of a grave and her bones lay in a heap when discovered. However, we do know that Neolithic communities interred their dead in the Gop Cave rock shelter (which actually consists of several low cave passages) above Prestatyn, as bones belonging to at least fourteen people were found here by William Boyd-Dawkins at the end of the nineteenth century. The bones were tightly-packed in a drystone-walled cist built against the back wall of the shelter; sherds of Neolithic Peterborough

Ware pottery, a polished flint knife, a few white quartz pebbles, and two 'belt-sliders' made of jet were found mixed in with the bones. Radiocarbon dating of the bones suggest a date range of around 3500–2900, and its wide date-span indicates that the cave was used as a Neolithic sepulchre for several centuries, with perhaps only special members of Neolithic communities afforded the privilege of burial here. Although no Mesolithic bones have been recovered from within the rock shelter, Late Mesolithic microliths have been recovered from around Gop Cave, suggesting that it was also utilised in some way by earlier hunter-gatherer communities in this area.

I should also mention that Gop Cave is located immediately below Gop Cairn, which is one of the most impressive and mysterious prehistoric monuments in Britain. This massive stone mound or barrow measures 70 by 100 metres in plan and reaches around 14 metres in height. Its true purpose continues to elude us. Boyd Dawkins sank a shaft through the centre of the mound and dug two tunnels through its base, but unfortunately he did not find any evidence that the huge cairn had been raised over human burials. It seems unlikely (but not impossible) that any human remains will ever be recovered from Gop Cairn. Although it has not been proved, it does seem probable that the cairn is somehow associated with the burials in Gop Cave and dates to the later Neolithic, or maybe even the Early Bronze Age. John Barnatt and Mark Edmonds have plausibly suggested that the cairn may actually have been built in order to draw people's attention to this important – and perhaps earlier – burial site which lay just below the cairn. As they point out, seen from a distance the cairn and the limestone outcrop in which Gop Cave is located 'become integrated, giving the appearance of a far more substantial monument'.

Moving up the coast to the Great Orme, which as we saw in Chapter 3 is the location of the important Upper Palaeolithic site of Kendrick's Cave, there is also the Lloches yr Afr rockshelter to consider. Chewed bones found in the cave reveal that it was first used by Palaeolithic hyenas, but shortly after 8000 BC, Mesolithic people moved in, leaving behind flint tools and animal and fish bones from their meals. A hearth on which they might have cooked their meals was also found, alongside which was a large hole that may originally have held a stake or post on which they cooked their food. The most mysterious find from the rockshelter was a cache of white quartz pebbles that had probably been collected from the nearby beach. It is not beyond the bounds of possibility that these were believed to possess 'magic' powers of some sort, as white quartz is often found at later prehistoric religious monuments such as stone circles.

The Rhuddlan Mesolithic 'Base Camp'

Martin Bell has plausibly argued that the evidence from Nant Hall Road probably indicates that both Late Mesolithic and Early Neolithic groups were briefly but repeatedly coming to this part of the Welsh coast from seasonal base camps to exploit its resources, during which time they lived in temporary camps that were only occupied for days or weeks. He has further credibly argued that 'The only really likely candidate for a [Mesolithic] base camp in the area, with longer-term, but not necessarily sedentary use, and the broader range of activities which that implies, is the excavated complex of sites at Rhuddlan'.

The Mesolithic sites at Rhuddlan were excavated between 1969 and 1978, and cover an area of land measuring some 8 hectares, which surrounds the impressive castle. This was built by Edward I in the late thirteenth century, as he began his campaign to wrest control of northern Wales from its native rulers. Many hundreds of Mesolithic stone tools were recovered from these sites. These date from both the Early and Late Mesolithic, although the majority of the Late Mesolithic tools were found at the site at Hendre. For the most part, the Mesolithic people at Rhuddlan had used chert and flint to make their tools, with the former probably collected from the scree slopes that lie below the limestone cliffs found in the Vale of Clwyd, and the latter, obtained from local beaches or inland glacial drift deposits. Microliths were ubiquitous on the site, with scrapers also well represented amongst the lithic assemblage; also included are knives, blades, piercers, awls and many 'retouched' (deliberately modified) lithics of uncertain function. One of these pieces, however, bears a distinctive gloss or polish along with damage on one of its edges, and archaeological experiments with other lithics suggest that it is quite likely that this artefact was used in plant-gathering. John Manley and Elizabeth Healey have plausibly suggested that the microliths found at Hendre 'could be seen as arrowheads being prepared for the next season's hunting in the hills', while the scrapers may have been used to make the shafts in which these were fixed. As well as perhaps being used as woodworking tools, the Mesolithic scrapers found at Rhuddlan are likely to have also been used in the preparation of hides and in the working of antlers.

Possible evidence of the existence of former Mesolithic dwellings was also uncovered by the archaeologists working at Rhuddlan, with the strongest hints in this regard coming from Site M (where the remains of a Norman church were also found). Here, they found a large flat-bottomed hollow containing several probable post-holes, and it is quite possible that these were all that was left of a wooden structure which had once been a home to some of Rhuddlan's Mesolithic occupants.

Undoubtedly, the most exciting and important Mesolithic evidence to come from Rhuddlan was a series of six sandstone pebbles featuring engraved decoration. The true significance of these mysterious stones is obviously lost to us, but it is probably unlikely that they represent the doodlings of Mesolithic hunter-gatherers with too much time on their hands. Although not all of the decorated pebbles were complete enough to allow suggestions to be put forward as to the possible meaning of the decoration seen on them, the three found at Sites E, M and T were. The example from Site M (which was recovered from the possible remains of the house mentioned above), is perhaps the most interesting of the three, as this has been plausibly interpreted as a possible anthropomorphic figurine on which clothes and different parts of the body are represented(a). It

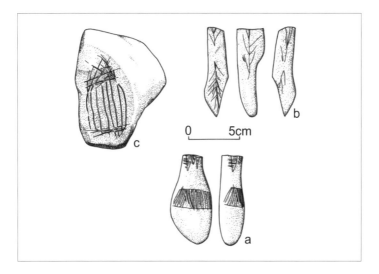

Decorated Mesolithic pebbles from Rhuddlan
(Redrawn after Lynch et al)

has been suggested that the decorated pebble found at Site E features a 'tree' motif(b) on its four main surfaces, while the motif seen on the one recovered from Site T (which was the only complete pebble among the six) has been interpreted as a Mesolithic fish trap, or alternatively a Mesolithic house(c). It may be interesting to note that among the remarkably well preserved Late Mesolithic fish traps discovered during development works in Dublin's docklands, there was an example which was similar in appearance to the motif seen on the pebble from Site T.

The evidence found at Rhuddlan strongly suggests that this was an important place of settlement throughout the Mesolithic period, and it does seem probable there were both Early and Late Mesolithic base camps located here. As Martin Bell has said in respect of this evidence:

> There are hints of timber structures [and the] Rhuddlan sites have larger numbers of lithics than others in the area and a more diverse range of artefact types suggesting the broader range of activities expected at a base camp.

He has also suggested that the Mesolithic 'artworks' found at Rhuddlan may lend further support to the idea that Mesolithic base camps once existed here, and says:

> It may not be too implausible to associate art with social communication and thus the activities associated with an aggregation camp where concentrations of people came together for periodic occupancy.

Whether Mesolithic people lived in these camps all year round, rather than on a seasonal basis, is a matter of debate. Some archaeologists favour the idea that hunter-gatherers would have lived in the uplands during the summer and come down to the Rhuddlan area in winter, as this would have been a time of year when there would have been good grazing areas for animals such as red deer, roe deer, wild boar and aurochs; they would also have been protected from the more severe conditions that prevailed in the uplands during the winter months. An alternative scenario, however, is that the river estuary area near which Rhuddlan is located provided enough resources for the establishment of permanent Mesolithic settlements, with the subsistence economies of these settlements perhaps further bolstered by small groups who split off from the main community at certain times of the year to hunt and gather in the lowlands and uplands.

We will move now to these uplands and the Mesolithic site found next to the Llyn Brenig reservoir in Denbighshire, which is located in the Brenig Valley in a wild and beautiful area of high moorland known as Mynydd Hiraethog.

Llyn Brenig

This site (Brenig 53) is located close to the Early Bronze Age barrow (Brenig 45) and impressive ring cairn (Brenig 44), which are situated at the edge of the reservoir. The site was located as a result of the excavation of these two monuments in 1973, when keen-eyed archaeologists spotted tell-tale changes in soil colour just to the east of Brenig 45. I should also point out that other fine examples of Early Bronze Age ritual and ceremonial monuments can be found along the Llyn Brenig Archaeological Trail, and the trail is highly recommended to readers. The fascinating remains of medieval *hafodau* (summer dwellings) dating to the fifteenth and sixteenth centuries, which were built by farming families who brought their livestock to graze in the uplands during the summer, can also be seen around Llyn Brenig.

In 1974 and 1975, archaeologists excavated the site and discovered the fragmentary remains of a Late Mesolithic hunting camp, as well as evidence of subsequent Neolithic activity. The Mesolithic hunters (probably mainly hunting deer) who lived here left behind various stone tools and associated waste when they moved on from this spot, which was probably not that different from how it appears today – although there would have been no reservoir filling the valley back then, of course! Birch and alder trees, however, may have grown in the valley bottom and along the banks of Afon Brenig, but it seems likely that the high moorland was essentially devoid of woodland, just as it is today. A group of hearths or fire-pits, around which the Mesolithic hunters had probably cooked food and kept warm, was also uncovered during the excavations, along with stakeholes that may represent a former windbreak, used to shelter the

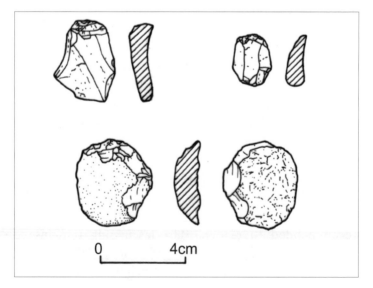

Mesolithic scrapers from Llyn Brenig
(Redrawn after Lynch)

fires. Several hazelnut shells found at the site also indicate that the Mesolithic occupants of Llyn Brenig had brought some supplies of food with them into the uplands. Likewise they must also have carried the raw materials for their tools to the site, as the flint and cherts from which they were made are absent from the Welsh uplands, although they could easily have been obtained from the coast and the Vale of Clwyd.

The Llyn Brenig Mesolithic site may have been occupied for only a matter of days or weeks by the Mesolithic group who left traces of their activities here, but it is perhaps possible that they may have stayed longer in this upland location than we might think. As the noted Welsh prehistorian Frances Lynch has pointed out, there is quite a wide variety of tool-types in the lithic assemblage at Llyn Brenig, suggesting a wide range of activities (including the preparation of skins) that would not perhaps be expected at a short-stay hunting camp. Thus, as she says, 'Maybe we have been too quick to assume that man would not wish to camp for long on the high moors, at least during the more clement weather'.

Ffynnon Beuno and Cae Gwyn

These two caves, which lie in close proximity to each other, lie just outside the village of Tremerchion, some seven miles south of Prestatyn, on the eastern side of the beautiful Vale of Clywd. Flint tools dating to the Early Upper Palaeolithic were recovered from both caves by the nineteenth-century antiquarians William Boyd Dawkins and Herbert Hicks, and those recovered from Ffynnon Beuno suggested that there may have been two phases of occupation here between 35,000 and 30,000 BP. Along with the lithics, many bones belonging to animals that would have roamed the Vale of Clwyd in the Upper Palaeolithic were found: animals such as lion, rhino, giant deer, bear and horse. The most common carnivore present in the faunal collection is the hyena, and the fact that many of the bones of the other animals show signs of gnawing indicates that both Ffynnon Beuno and Cae Gwyn were hyena dens in the Upper Palaeolithic.

Whether both caves were occupied at the same, or different times, is unknown, but it is not beyond the bounds of possibility that each cave was occupied by contemporary Upper Palaeolithic families who – given the close proximity of the caves to each other – would have had to have been on neighbourly terms! Alternatively, both caves may have been occupied by one large family or extended kin group, but it is probably more likely that the Upper Palaeolithic occupation of the two caves was not contemporaneous.

Anglesey/Ynys Môn

Anglesey is an island richly endowed with evidence of the many different prehistoric communities who lived here in the distant past. If this evidence is presenting us with a true picture of Anglesey's prehistoric story, then it seems that the first prehistoric communities to live on the island were groups of Mesolithic hunter-gatherers, although we should perhaps not totally discount an Upper Palaeolithic presence on the island also. I say 'island', but it was not until around 4000 BC that Anglesey was finally cut off from mainland Wales by the post-glacial rise in sea level.

It would be fair to say that the Mesolithic people of Anglesey have been somewhat overshadowed by their Neolithic, Bronze, and Iron Age successors, who left many impressive and visible reminders of their lives on the island (the same could be said for many other areas of Britain). However, important sites such as the one discovered beneath an Early Bronze Age kerbed cairn on the rocky headland of Trwyn Du, Aberffraw, ensure that Anglesey's ancient hunter-gatherer communities are not completely forgotten. Small scatters of Mesolithic lithics have been found at a number places on the island, but the largest group of Mesolithic flints yet found on Anglesey was recovered from the old land surface beneath the cairn.

Today, Trwyn Du is on the coast but the Mesolithic people who occupied the site for an unkown length of time some 5,000 years earlier (around 7000 BC) would probably have been two to three miles from the sea. Several microliths, scrapers, blades and two finely-made stone axes were recovered, along with large quantities of debitage (waste material) relating to the production of these tools. Two small pits were also identified at the site, and these may once have held posts that formed part of a windbreak or maybe an even more substantial structure. Interestingly, also found in the lithic assemblage was a single flake from a Neolithic polished stone axe that had been made of stone quarried from the Mynydd Rhiw axe factory in Llŷn. This small piece of evidence indicates that later Neolithic people were also making stone tools at the site, although it would probably be pushing it too far to suggest that they were descended from the earlier Mesolithic tool-makers of Trwyn Du.

An intriguing possibility raised by the close association of the Mesolithic site and the Early Bronze Age cairn is that the people responsible for the construction of the cairn deliberately located it at Trwyn Du because it was a sacred site, perhaps associated with ancestral figures from the Mesolithic. Such an idea may seem far-fetched and fanciful, and the juxtaposition of the Mesolithic site and the cairn may be nothing more than a happy coincidence. However, further possible evidence of how later prehistoric communities in Wales may have deliberately built their religious monuments on earlier hunter-gatherer sites has been found at the Bryn Celli Ddu Late Neolithic passage grave (built around 3000 BC) on Anglesey. The archaeologist, Wifred James Hemp, who excavated at Bryn Celli Ddu between 1925 and 1929, discovered post-holes in front of the tomb's entrance, which had once probably held an alignment of five fairly large posts (about 6 ins in diameter).

It is perhaps also possible, as Hemp notes in the excavation report, that they once formed part of a wattle screen. Whatever the case, it is clear that the wooden posts that had originally stood in these post-holes had been erected in the Mesolithic, as pine charcoal from two of them has recently been dated to 5990–5730 BC. Intriguingly, just to the north-east of the row of posts Hemp found a shallow pit in which lay the skeleton of an ox, and although the date of this bovine burial is unclear, Hemp mentions that it lay in a symmetrical position on the axis of the forecourt and that '[its] body had been doubled up and crammed into as small a hole as possible, the head twisted round towards the entrance to the tomb'. This therefore suggests that the burial is contemporary with the construction or use of the passage grave, although we cannot rule out the possibility that the ox actually dates to the Mesolithic, and its close proximity to the postholes is worth bearing in mind in this regard.

Of course, the Mesolithic posts would have long since disappeared by the time the passage grave came to be built, and thus it appears likely that the close proximity of the former to the latter may again be nothing more than mere chance. However, I still wonder at how the post-holes are located in the forecourt of Bryn Celli Ddu, almost directly opposite the entrance into the tomb. This perhaps suggests that at the least, the builders of the passage grave were aware that this area had once been the scene of Mesolithic

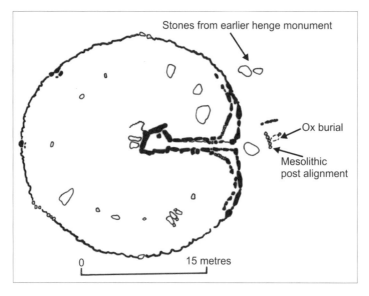

Plan of Bryn Celli Ddu Passage Grave,
Mesolithic monument and ox burial
(Redrawn after O'Kelly)

ritual activity. Could it even be possible that the location of
the former Mesolithic structure was somehow still marked
in the landscape some 3,000 years later, when Bryn Celli
Ddu came to be built? Admittedly, this is a very remote
possibility, and, perhaps it is more likely that the evidence
found at Bryn Celli Ddu provides us with a similar scenario
to that found at Stonehenge: in 1966, three large pits in a
row came to light at the famous monument during the
construction of the first car park, and a further pit located
around 100 metres to the east was revealed when the visitor
centre was built in 1988. These pits had once held huge pine
posts about 3 feet in diameter, and they must also have
reached a decent height. Subsequent radiocarbon dates
obtained from material found in the pits revealed, somewhat
remarkably, that they had been erected in the Mesolithic

between 8500 and 7650 BC. As Francis Pryor has rightly pointed out, it is hard to see what practical function these huge posts could have served, and therefore, as he has said, they must surely have had a ritual or religious function (it could also be possible that the posts were carved and painted – as perhaps those at Bryn Celli Ddu were). He is likely to be right in his assertion that these posts prove 'that Stonehenge and its immense ritual landscape was positioned within a sacred landscape that was already four thousand years old when the first Neolithic monuments appeared on the scene'.

It is now known that the builders of Bryn Celli Ddu directly orientated its passage so that the rays of the rising midsummer sun shone down it to illuminate the dark reaches of the inner chamber in which the dead were laid to rest. Interestingly, the hunter-gatherers who erected the wooden structure at Bryn Celli Ddu, and perhaps also buried an ox, may also have incorporated a celestial alignment into their monument. However, if they did, it seems that rather than venerating the sun, as the builders of Bryn Celli Ddu appear to have done, they instead worshipped its cold counterpart, as it has been suggested by some archaeologists and archaeoastronomers that its posts may have marked different rising positions of the moon. However, Martin J. Powell, who is an expert on astronomical alignments in Welsh Neolithic and Bronze Age monuments, feels that although it is not impossible, it is unlikely that the posts have any lunar connection.

As well as at Prestatyn, several shell middens have also been found on Anglesey at places such as Cerrig Mawr and Newborough Warren on the west coast. However, as far as I am aware, none of the shell middens has been conclusively dated to the Mesolithic, and thus they could be much later in date, as shellfish would also have provided sustenance for many people of later periods. A good example of one such later midden is provided by the substantial example found at a Romano-British roundhouse at Penmon, but nonetheless, it still seems likely that several of Anglesey's shell middens were left behind by Mesolithic groups who once occupied the island.

Llŷn and Bardsey Island/Ynys Enlli

A number of Mesolithic sites have also been found around the glorious coastline of Llŷn, with the most recent coming to light on the famous Bardsey Island (*Ynys Enlli*), which sits in splendid and serene isolation at the peninsula's south-western tip. Although the results of the archaeological work at the site (carried out by a team led by Mark Edmonds, an expert on prehistoric stoneworking) have not yet been fully published, it can be said that as a result of ploughing in fields located at the northern end of the island, a scatter of various Mesolithic tools and working debris has been recovered. This points to the existence of a former Mesolithic occupation site on the island, and it appears that, on the basis of the lithic types included in the assemblage, this occupation probably took place in the Late Mesolithic period between 7000 and 4000 BC. It will be interesting to read the final report on this fascinating and important site.

Facing Bardsey Island on the south-western tip of Llŷn is Pared Llechymenyn, which is a small rocky cove with high, sheer cliffs. Evidence for Mesolithic activity in the form of three flint scatters containing several tools was found on top of the cliffs on the south-eastern side of the cove. Two were recovered from the exposed faces of 'teracettes' in a steep slope on the cliff edge, and the third was discovered when an adjoining field was ploughed. It is likely that the finds are not in situ and have slipped down towards the cliff edge over time from a more extensive area of occupation that is located in this field. Therefore, it would be interesting to see what turned up from this location if it were to be the subject of a more extensive future archaeological investigation.

Five finely-made, large Mesolithic blades and a couple of small flint flakes were also found not far from Pared Llechymenyn on the edge of a cliff at Parwyd, Uwchmynydd, which lies about two miles south-west of the lovely coastal hamlet of Aberdaron. All of the blades are of the same material and were probably made from a tuff which was sourced from the immediate locality. Two examples showed signs of wear on their corners, indicating that they were used as awls or piercing instruments. Whether further evidence for Mesolithic activity exists at Parwyd is unknown, but it is certainly a possibility.

Moving from the peninsula's end and following the broad sweep of Porth Neigwl (or Hell's Mouth as it is called in English), we come to the two headlands of Pencilan and Trwyn yr Wylfa, between which is located the picturesque beach at Porth Ceriad.

A Mesolithic flint scatter was found on Pencilan near Fronheulog Farm, but the most important Mesolithic evidence from this part of the peninsula was found at Bryn Refail Farm in the hamlet of Bwlch Tocyn, which lies about a mile south from the popular seaside resort of Abersoch. Maurice Ridgeway and Geoffrey Leach carried out limited archaeological work at the farm in 1939, finding evidence of Late Mesolithic flint working in the ploughed fields around the farm and in a small test pit they opened up. Further Mesolithic lithics were found as surface finds at the farm during the Second World War, but it was not until April 1946 that the archaeologists returned to Bryn Refail Farm to cut a long and narrow trench (30 feet long and 18 inches wide) that linked up with the test pit they had dug seven years previously. They recovered a lithic assemblage consisting of some 1,700 lithics, and although most of these were small waste flakes and small chippings from stone tool production, eleven flint cores were found, along with thirty definite tools. Included in the stone tool assemblage were several microliths and scrapers and flakes with deliberate modification or 'retouch' on their edges, and amongst the lithics found as surface finds in the neighbouring fields was a 'hand pick'. The Mesolithic people from the Bryn Refail site probably gathered the flint nodules that provided the raw material for their stone tools from the nearby beaches at Porth Ceriad and Porth Mawr, which today are crowded with holidaymakers in the summer months. The three winkle shells found at the site also reveal how the Bryn Refail hunter-gatherers were gathering food resources from these beaches.

Doubtless, there are more remnants of prehistoric hunter-gatherer life waiting to be discovered not only in Llŷn, but right across the captivating landscapes of Wales. To some, these remnants may seem small and insignificant in light of the cultural achievements of Wales' later prehistoric peoples. However, speaking for myself, I feel that they can only help to shed fascinating light on the lives of communities whose ancient way of life was ultimately doomed to extinction with the arrival of farming on the shores of Wales.

That, however, is another story ...

Glossary

Acheulian
The name given to the Lower Palaeolithic stone tool 'industry' associated with early humans (particularly *Homo erectus*) that first emerged in Africa over 1.5 million years ago and which lasted until around 300,000 years ago.

Burin
A stone tool with a chisel-like edge – from the French word meaning 'cold chisel'. They would have been used for engraving and carving, wood bone and antler.

Busked Burin
Similar to a burin but with a notch removed at one end.

Cist
Stone box-like graves usually formed of four side-slabs and a capstone, which were a feature of both the prehistoric and medieval periods in Britain.

Cortical Flake
A stone tool removed from a core of raw material (e.g. flint), which, on one side is still covered by the original surface or 'cortex' of this raw material.

Cthonic
Spirits or deities of the Underworld/Otherworld. The word 'Cthonic' comes from *Khthón*, the Greek word for earth.

Ethnographic Record
Information collected by ethnographers/anthropologists on past and present human societies around the world.

Lithics
Archaeological term for stone tools and the associated waste material from their production (with the latter sometimes referred to as 'debitage') that is found in the archaeological record.

Microwear Analysis	The scientific study of wear on damage on stone tools which provides valuable information on how they were used in the past.
Palaeoanthropology	The study of ancient humans and their development through the fossil evidence found in the archaeological record.
Palaeo-ecological	Scientific analysis of fossil organisms to recreate ecosystems of the past.
Parietal	Technical term for prehistoric cave art.
Sherds	Archaeological term for pieces of broken pottery vessels from both the prehistoric and historic periods.
Steatopygia	An extreme accumulation of fat on the buttocks.
Stratigraphy	A branch of geology that studies rock layers and which archaeologists have borrowed, realising that it can give them 'relative' dates for layers on archaeological sites.
Taurodontism	A condition found in the molar teeth of modern humans, whereby the body of the tooth and pulp cavity is enlarged vertically at the expense of the roots. Taurodontism is also a characteristic feature of Neanderthal skeletons.

Select Bibliography

Aldhouse-Green, S., *Ice Age Hunters: Neanderthals and Early Modern Hunters in Wales* (National Museum of Wales, 1991)

Aldhouse-Green, S., *Paviland Cave and the 'Red Lady': A Definitive Report* (Western Academic & Specialist Press, 2000)

Aldhouse-Green, S. and Pettit, P., 'Paviland Cave: contextualizing the "Red Lady"', in *Antiquity* 72, 756–772 (1998)

Aldhouse-Green, S. H. R., Whittle, A. W. R, Allen, J. R. L, Caseldine, A. E., Culver, S. J., Day, M. H., Lundquist, J. and Upton. D., 'Prehistoric Human Footprints from the Severn Estuary at Uskmouth and Magor Pill, Gwent, Wales', in *Archaeologia Cambrensis* CXLI, 14–55 (1992)

Bahn, P., *Journey through the Ice Age* (Seven Dials, 1997)

Barton, N., *Ice Age Britain* (BT Batsford, 2005)

Barton, R. N. E, Berridge, P. J., Walker, M. J. C. and Bevins, R. E., 'Persistent Places in the Mesolithic Landscape: an Example from the Black Mountain Uplands of South Wales', in *Proceedings of the Prehistoric Society* 61, 81–116 (1995)

Bell, M., *Prehistoric Coastal Communities: The Mesolithic in western Britain* (Council for British Archaeology Research Report 149, 2007)

Bradley, R., *An Archaeology of Natural Places* (Routledge, 2000)

Chamberlain, A. T. and Williams, J. P. 2000, *A Gazetteer of Welsh Caves, Fissures and Rock Shelters Containing Human Remains. Capra* 2 available at – http://capra.group.shef.ac.uk/2/wales.html

Clark, J. G. D., *Excavations at Starr Carr: an Early Mesolithic site at Seamer near Scarborough, North Yorkshire* (Cambridge University Press, 1971)

Council for British Archaeology, Wales, Newsletter 24 (Autumn 2002): A Later Mesolithic assemblage on Bardsey Island

Current Archaeology Magazine 2010 (248). 'Britain's Oldest House', 7

Current Archaeology Magazine 2011 (259). 'Welsh Cave Art', 8–9

David, A., *Palaeolithic and Mesolithic Settlement in Wales, with special reference to Dyfed* (British Archaeological Reports 448, 2007)

Gaffney, V., 'Not Waving but Drowning: the lands that Europe lost', in *The Archaeologist* 80, 18–19 (2011)

Gordon-Williams, J. P., 'The Nab Head Chipping Floor', in *Archaeologia Cambrensis* VI, 86–110 (1926)

Green, S. H, 'The first Welshman: excavations at Pontnewydd', in *Antiquity* LV, 184–195 (1981)

Green, S., and Walker, E., *Ice Age Hunters: Neanderthals and Early Modern Hunters in Wales* (Amgueddfa Genedlaethol Cymru/National Museum of Wales 1991)

Higham, T., Stringer, C. and Douka, K., 'Dating Europe's oldest modern humans', in *British Archaeology* 122, 25–29 (2012)

Hoyle, B., 'Cave Artwork shines a light on prehistoric playpens', in *The Times* (30 September 2011)

Jacobi, R. M. and Higham, T. G. F., 'The "Red Lady" ages gracefully: new ultrafiltration AMS determinations from Paviland', in *Journal of Human Evolution* 55, 898–907 (2008)

Lacaille, A. D. and Grimes, W. F., 'The Prehistory of Caldey', in *Archaeologia Cambrensis* CIV, 85–165 (1956)

Lynch, F., *Prehistoric Anglesey* (The Anglesey Antiquarian Society, 1970)

Lynch, F., Aldhouse-Green, S. and Davies, J. L., *Prehistoric Wales* (Sutton, 2000)

Manley, J. and Healey, E., 'Excavations at Hendre, Rhuddlan', in *Archaeologia Cambrensis* CXXXI, 18–48 (1982)

Miles, D., *The Tribes of Britain* (Phoenix, 2006)

Moss, S., 'The Secrets of Paviland Cave', *Guardian* (25 April 2011)

North, F. J., *Sunken Cities: Some legends of the coast and lakes of Wales* (University of Wales Press, 1957)

Oliver, N., *A History of Ancient Britain* (Weidenfeld & Nicolson, 2011)

Parfitt, S., Stuart, T., Stringer, C. and Preece, R., 'Pakefield: a weekend to remember', in *British Archaeology* 86, 19–27 (2006)

Parfitt, S., Ashton, N. and Lewis, S., 'Happisburgh', in *British Archaeology* 114, 15–23 (2010)

Pitts, M., and Roberts, M., *Fairweather Eden* (Arrow, 1998)

Pettit, P., 'Odd Man Out: Neanderthals and Modern Humans', in

British Archaeology 51, 8–13 (2000)

Pryor, F., *Britain BC: Life in Britain and Ireland before the Romans* (Harper Collins, 2003)

Quinnell, H., Blockley, M. R. and Berridge, P., *Excavations at Rhuddlan, Clwyd 1969–73, Mesolithic to Medieval* (Council for British Archaeology, Research Report 95, 1994)

Ridgeway, M. H. and Leach, G. B., 'Prehistoric Flint Workshop Site near Abersoch, Caernarvonshire' in *Archaeologia Cambrensis* XCIX, 78–84 (1947)

Ripoll, S., Muñoz, F., Bahn, P. and Pettitt, P., 'Palaeolithic Cave Engravings at Creswell Crags, England', in *Proceedings of the Prehistoric Society* 70, 93–106

Savory, H. N., 'Excavations at the Hoyle, Tenby, in 1968, in *Archaeologia Cambrensis* CXXI, 18–34 (1973)

Seiveking, G. de G., 'The Kendrick's Cave Mandible', *British Museum Quarterly* 35, 230–250 (1971)

Solecki, R. S., *Shanidar: the Humanity of Neanderthal man* (Allen Lane, The Penguin Press, 1972)

Smith, G., *North-West Wales Lithics Scatters Project: Evaluation of the Early Prehistoric Landscape through Lithic Finds* (GAT Project G1590) (2001)

Sommer, M., 'An amusing account of a cave in Wales': William Buckland (1784–1856) and the Red Lady of Paviland', in *British Journal for the History of Science* 37, 53–74 (2004)

Thomas, J., *Rethinking the Neolithic*, (Cambridge University Press, 1991)

Thorpe, L. T. (trans.), Gerald of Wales. *The Journey through Wales/The Description of Wales* (Penguin, 1978)

Tyldesley, J., *The* Bout Coupé *Handaxe: A typological problem* (British Archaeological Reports 170, 1987)

White, R. B., 'Excavations at Trwyn Du, Anglesey, 1974', in *Archaeologia Cambrensis* CXXVII, 16–39 (1978)

Wynn, T. W., 'Handaxe Enigmas', in *World Archaeology* 27, 10–24 (1995)

Acknowledgements

Many people have made generous contributions to this book, and in particular, I would like to express my gratitude to George Nash and Steve Clarke for all their help. I must also thank: Ken Murphy/Dyfed Archaeological Trust, Joyce Tyldesley, Deborah Tilley, Dai Barnaby, Chris Elphick, Gavin H. Evans/ Carmarthenshire County Museum, Rod Ward, Eirian Evans, Stephen McKay, Noel Walley, Martin J. Powell, Steve Burrow, Adrian Pingstone, Angharad Stockwell and Nina Steele/ Gwynedd Archaeological Trust, and Emma Turner/Clwyd-Powys Archaeological Trust.

I would also like to thank Medwyn Parry and Penny Icke/The Royal Commission on the Ancient and Historical Monuments of Wales, and Nick Barton.

Special thanks to Neil Oliver for allowing us to use the quote from *A History of Ancient Britain* on the front cover of this book.

Finally, thanks also to Myrddin ap Dafydd, Jen Llywelyn (thanks for the suggestions), and all the team at Gwasg Carreg Gwalch.

Further books of interest

Visit our website for further information:
www.carreg-gwalch.com

Orders can be placed on our
On-line Shop